An Introductory Guide to SPSS® for Windows®

SECOND EDITION

For my parents, Norman and Edith

An Introductory Guide to SPSS® for Windows®

SECOND EDITION

Eric L. Einspruch
RMC Research Corporation

SAGE Publications
Thousand Oaks ▪ London ▪ New Delhi

Screen shot on the cover was taken with the permission of SPSS, Inc.

For information:

Sage Publications, Inc.
2455 Teller Road
Thousand Oaks, California 91320
E-mail: order@sagepub.com

Sage Publications Ltd.
1 Oliver's Yard
55 City Road
London EC1Y 1SP
United Kingdom

Sage Publications India Pvt. Ltd.
B-42, Panchsheel Enclave
Post Box 4109
New Delhi 110 017 India

Printed in the United States of America

Library of Congress Cataloging-in-Publication Data

Einspruch, Eric L.
An introductory guide to SPSS® for Windows® / Eric L. Einspruch.—2nd ed.
    p. cm.
Includes bibliographical references and index.
ISBN 1-4129-0415-3 (Paper)
    1. SPSS for Windows. 2. Social sciences—
Statistical methods—Computer programs. I. Title.
HA32.E446 2005
519.5′078′553—dc22

                                    2004024122

This book is printed on acid-free paper.

05   06   07   08   09   10   9   8   7   6   5   4   3   2   1

Acquisitions Editor:	Lisa Cuevas Shaw
Editorial Assistant:	Margo Beth Crouppen
Production Editor:	Melanie Birdsall
Copy Editor:	Carla Freeman
Typesetter:	C&M Digitals (P) Ltd.
Proofreader:	Teresa Herlinger
Cover Designer:	Glenn Vogel

Contents

Acknowledgments

I owe a debt of gratitude to many people who have directly or indirectly contributed to this book. Arthur Gutman of the Florida Institute of Technology suggested that I write this book. C. Deborah Laughton, formerly of Sage Publications, was instrumental in bringing the first edition of this book to fruition, and Lisa Cuevas Shaw helped bring forth this second edition. Several authors granted me permission to quote examples from their work. Reviewers of drafts of the manuscript provided helpful insights and suggestions. SPSS, Inc. was accessible and provided me with information about updates to their software. Thank you to each of you.

I would also like to express my sincere appreciation to the many family members, friends, colleagues, and students who have encouraged and supported my interest in research and statistics, and who have taught me much over the years. In addition, I wish to acknowledge the many people with whom I have worked who have applied research and evaluation results to improving the lives of those they serve. I am ever grateful to you.

CHAPTER 1

Introduction

This book is designed to provide the reader with an introduction to one of the most popular computer programs for data analysis: the Statistical Package for the Social Sciences (SPSS) for Windows. This computer software provides a comprehensive set of flexible tools that can be used to accomplish a wide variety of data analysis tasks. The book covers the fundamentals of SPSS, and by the time they reach the end of the book, readers will have a working knowledge of how to use SPSS to read, manage, and analyze data. I have written this book using SPSS Version 12.0, which runs on the Microsoft Windows operating system. However, the material covered in this book is applicable to earlier (and I predict later) Windows versions of SPSS, although the pull-down menus and dialog boxes will not exactly match the figures in this book.

The ability to conduct research is an important skill. If you are interested in learning about service delivery, client perceptions, or the knowledge, attitudes, or behaviors of a group of persons, then you need fundamental skills in research design, data collection and analysis, and report writing. This is particularly true for those interested in program evaluation and for those engaged in collecting data to contribute to policy or decision making (perhaps in support of ongoing program improvement).

When conducting research or evaluation, a suitable data collection instrument must be designed and administered to some number of subjects (from as few as one or two dozen to as many as several hundred thousand). The data, once collected, must be analyzed. In the past, data analysis was a tedious process done by hand (often at least three times for each analysis: once to get the answer, once to check the answer, and once to reconcile differences between the first two answers due to error in the calculations). And that was just for the first analysis, perhaps a simple one such as the computation of frequency distributions. Then came more calculations of descriptive and inferential statistics.

Fortunately, we live in an age when high-speed computers take the tedium out of statistical computation (and reduce the likelihood of errors), allowing the calculation and recalculation of statistics in a brief period of time. The ability of the computer to perform these calculations quickly and accurately allows a researcher to spend his or her time searching for patterns in the data and answering questions of interest, rather than on the mechanics of computation.

This book is ideally suited to a one-semester introductory course on the use of computers in research, for someone learning SPSS on his or her own, or for someone who is returning to the SPSS software and is in need of a refresher. I have assumed that readers are already familiar with the material normally covered in a first course in statistics (or are currently becoming familiar with this material). Readers who wish to brush up on their statistics are encouraged to see Sirkin (1999), while readers who wish to explore the field of statistics in greater depth are referred to Gibbons (1985), Gibbons and Chakraborti (1992), Hays (1991), Kirk (1995), and Pedhazur (1997).

I have written this book in as nontechnical a manner as possible so that it is an easy-to-use introduction to the power of SPSS. In doing so, I have pointed straight to the fundamental concepts of the software. However, please be aware that SPSS is capable of far more than what is covered in this book. Once you have become familiar with the software, you can use the SPSS manuals to increase your skills and understanding. In fact, you may find it helpful to keep the manuals (available on the CD that came with your copy of SPSS) nearby as you read this book, so that they may serve to expand on the topics that are introduced here. You will also find it helpful to sit at the computer as you read this book, trying the skills that are being discussed.

Before we continue, let me say a few things about computers. First, *feel free to experiment*. Try the procedures that are presented and have fun. Don't worry, you are not going to break anything, as long as you don't hit the machine with a hammer, toss it off the desk, or anything like that. Sure, you will make mistakes. Everyone does at one time or another, even the best SPSS users. So don't be afraid to try to do the work we are discussing—if things get bad, you can always start over. Just be sure to remember to save your work frequently.

SPSS is available on a variety of platforms. People with access to mainframe computers have the capability of analyzing immense datasets with blinding speed. Mainframe computers may be accessed through workplace terminals or, in some cases, via modem from an outside location (which provides the convenience of working from home or some other site). Others have access to SPSS on personal computers and thus the convenience of performing data analysis on their own stand-alone machines. The information in this book is presented from a Windows perspective, and I have assumed that readers already have a working familiarity with Windows operations (such as clicking to select an item, double-clicking to choose an item, entering text and selecting options in dialog boxes, switching between different windows, etc.). Readers who are in need of a refresher on the Windows operating system are encouraged to review manuals or other books on the subject. Throughout this book, I have used **bold** text to indicate operations or choices that the reader will need to make when running SPSS (for example, when I say something like "From the **File** pull-down menu . . ." I mean that you should click on the **File** menu at the top of the SPSS screen).

The SPSS skills covered in this book are introduced and illustrated with sample programs. Each program is designed to analyze data that have been gathered to answer a research question. The output from the program is then presented and interpreted to yield an answer to that question. Exercises are included in several chapters, and solutions are provided in Appendix A. Thus, it is my hope to provide a hands-on approach leading to mastery of basic SPSS skills.

In Chapter 2, we will look at how to organize data in a manner suitable for analysis by SPSS. There will be a review of variables and values, and a discussion of how to code data. The use of a codebook will be illustrated to record, for future reference, how data have been defined. Finally, some thought will be given to data entry.

In Chapter 3, we will begin to use SPSS. First, we will look at the way in which SPSS operates. The different files with which we will be working (syntax, data, output, and chart files) and their relationships to one another will be introduced. By the end of this chapter, readers will have conducted their first analyses using SPSS and viewed the results of the analyses.

It is typically necessary to manipulate data before analyzing them. Data may need to be recoded, computations may need to be made, new variables may need to be created, and certain records may need to be selected from the dataset. These tasks will be covered in Chapter 4.

Chapter 5 will introduce some intermediate concepts regarding data files. We will look at how to read data files that were not created in SPSS (such as those that have been saved as simple text files). We will also examine how to append data files (that is, to add cases from one file to another) and how to merge data files (that is, to add variables from one file to another).

The power of SPSS lies in its ability to perform complex statistical operations on large datasets, saving the researcher countless hours of computations. Chapter 6 illustrates the use of SPSS pull-down menus to perform the statistical analyses typically covered in a first statistics course. Each method will be introduced by a statement of a research question, followed by a discussion of how to use SPSS to conduct the analysis. Output from the analysis will be presented and interpreted, and an answer to the research question will be given.

In addition to using pull-down menus to conduct an analysis, users have the ability to write programs using SPSS syntax to manipulate and analyze data. Indeed, many of SPSS's capabilities may be accessed only through the use of syntax. Chapter 7 introduces basic SPSS programming skills, taking the reader beyond the features available via the pull-down menus.

Chapter 8 provides some direction for next steps in your study of SPSS. First, there is a discussion of how to get help in SPSS. Next, I encourage readers to make use of the wealth of information available in the SPSS manuals. The content and the structure of the manuals are reviewed, and examples are provided in which topics not covered in this book are researched using the manuals. This discussion will help readers become successful at using the manuals as reference tools. Finally, I present some topics that will be of interest to those who wish to further develop their SPSS skills.

Some concluding remarks are made in Chapter 9. You will be well on your way to becoming a skilled SPSS user once you have reached this point. I hope that you will have also sensed the adventure and fun of using SPSS.

CHAPTER 2

Creating Datasets

Chapter Purpose

This chapter introduces fundamental concepts of data files.

Chapter Goal

To help readers gain knowledge about how to structure a data file and enter data.

Chapter Glossary

Codebook: A record of the details of a dataset.

Fixed-Length Flat File: Data organization in which each line of data has the same number of columns and the data for a particular variable always appear in the same column.

Missing Value: Out-of-range value assigned to represent missing data for a variable.

Variable: Something that can be observed and that can take on more than one value.

Data must be organized in a certain way for SPSS to be able to read them. While this is not a difficult matter, it must be done correctly. There are easy and difficult, efficient and inefficient ways to approach the creation of datasets. Since our primary interest is in spending time finding the answers to research and evaluation questions, we will strive to make the task of creating a dataset as simple as possible.

It is always preferable to plan a dataset before launching into data collection and data entry. What experimental design has been used for the study? What variables have been measured, based on the research questions and experimental design? What values can these variables assume? Will the data for each person fit on one line in the dataset, or will multiple lines be needed for each person? How can the data be coded in order to make data entry easier (and computer storage more efficient)? The answers to these questions will help determine the structure of the dataset.

The details about a dataset are commonly recorded in a *codebook,* since it is a rare person who can remember the details about the data that have been collected for every project he or she has worked on (or who can remember the details of any one project for any length of time). The codebook may be only one page long, or it may occupy an entire volume, depending on the structure of the dataset. Ultimately, the codebook is a map that serves as a guide for reading the data (and remembering their contents).

DEFINING DATA FILES AND CODING DATA

Lewis-Beck (1995) presented a hypothetical dataset of results from a study of influences on academic ability. In his example, the Academic Affairs Office of Wintergreen College commissioned a study to investigate the determinants of success on a first-year entrance examination. A sample of 50 first-year students was drawn from a list of all 500 first-year students, which was provided by the registrar, and each student in the sample was assigned a unique *respondent number.* Student scores were obtained on a 100-item entrance examination of *academic ability* (scores were simply the number of items correct on the examination). In addition, a 36-item survey was administered to students in face-to-face interviews. This survey provided information on several key variables, including *parent education* (the average number of years of schooling for each parent), *student motivation* (based on the response to a question about whether or not the student would be willing to spend extra hours studying), *religion* (Catholic, Protestant, or Jewish), *gender* (male or female), and the *community type* from which the student came (urban or rural). Finally, students' admissions materials were accessed, including the academic advisor's handwritten comments assessing each student's likelihood to succeed in college. These comments were grouped into a variable called *advisor evaluation* (with the categories of "likely to succeed," "could succeed or could fail," and "likely to fail").

Thus, there are eight variables in this hypothetical study (which were placed in the following order in the dataset):

O Respondent number

O Academic ability

O Parent education

O Student motivation

O Advisor evaluation

O Religious affiliation

O Gender

O Community type

A *variable* is something that can be observed and that can take on more than one *value* (for example, in this study, community type is a variable that can take on one of two values: urban or rural). Earlier versions of SPSS were limited to variable names that were no more than eight characters long, and we needed to be creative and name our variables in a simple way. Lewis-Beck (1995) used the following names for the variables: Academic ability was named "aa," parent education was named "pe," student motivation was named "sm," advisor evalua-tion was named "ae," religious affiliation was named "r," gender was named "g," and community type was named "c." However, in the current version of SPSS, we are able to use longer variable names, so I have named respondent number "RespondentNumber" (SPSS does not allow the use of a space in the variable name). Fortunately, SPSS allows us to assign *labels* to our variables, so that it is easy to remember what they are, even if their names are brief and minimally descriptive.

In creating datasets, we frequently assign codes to the values of variables to make data entry easier and computer storage more effi-cient. For example, in the Wintergreen study, gender is a variable that can take on two values. These have been coded so that "0" represents "Male" and "1" represents "Female." Other codes could be used for these values (for example, "M" for "Male" and "F" for "Female"), but SPSS will not accept these values (called *alphanumeric* values because they use letters as well as numbers) for some analytic tasks.

As you begin to work with more and more datasets, you will find that it becomes increasingly difficult to remember how each one is structured.

It is therefore a good idea to record the coding scheme for the dataset. The following codebook (see Figure 2.1) has been created for the Wintergreen data, using the codes assigned by Lewis-Beck (1995).

Variable name:	RespondentNumber
Variable label:	Respondent Number
Values:	Sequential number of respondents 1 through 50
Variable name:	aa
Variable label:	Academic Ability
Values:	Number of items correct on 100-item entrance examination
Variable name:	pe
Variable label:	Parent Education
Values:	Average years of education for mother and father
Variable name:	sm
Variable label:	Student Motivation
Values and	0 Not willing
value labels:	1 Undecided
	2 Willing
Variable name:	ae
Variable label:	Advisor Evaluation
Values and	0 Fail
value labels:	1 Succeed or fail
	2 Succeed
Variable name:	r
Variable label:	Religious Affiliation
Values and	0 Catholic
value labels:	1 Protestant
	2 Jewish
Variable name:	g
Variable label:	Gender
Values and	0 Male
value labels:	1 Female
Variable name:	c
Variable label:	Community Type
Values and	0 Urban
value labels:	1 Rural

Figure 2.1   Codebook for the Wintergreen Study

In recording the data for this study, a dataset will be created in which one line will be entered for each student's data. Each line will exactly match all the other lines in structure, so that data for any one variable will always appear in the same column of the dataset. However, the data in each of the lines will be different from the others, since each contains the information for a different student. Thus, if the first student got 93 questions correct on the entrance examination, had parents who had an average of 19 years of schooling, was undecided about whether or not he would be willing to spend extra hours studying; was evaluated by the academic advisor as likely to succeed in college; was Catholic, male, and from an urban community; then the line of data (called a *record*) for this student would look like this:

RespondentNumber	aa	pe	sm	ae	r	g	c
01	93	19	1	2	0	0	1

Similarly, if the second student got 46 questions correct on the entrance examination, had parents who had an average of 12 years of schooling; was undecided about whether or not he would be willing to spend extra hours studying; was evaluated by the academic advisor as likely to succeed in college; was Catholic, male, and from an urban community; then the record for this person would look like this:

RespondentNumber	aa	pe	sm	ae	r	g	c
02	46	12	0	0	0	0	0

Together, the two records would look like this:

RespondentNumber	aa	pe	sm	ae	r	g	c
01	93	19	1	2	0	0	1
02	46	12	0	0	0	0	0

. . . and so on for the remaining students. This kind of data organization is called a *fixed-length flat file*, and it is characterized by every line having the same number of columns and the data for a particular variable always being in the same column. Each row is called a *record*, and in this example, each record represents the data for one student (or *case*). If there were quite a bit of data collected from each student, then each case might require more than one record in the dataset (in other words, it might take two or more lines of data for each student). The final dataset, with the information from all 50 students, appears as shown in Figure 2.2.

Respondent Number	aa	pe	sm	ae	r	g	c
01	93	19	1	2	0	0	1
02	46	12	0	0	0	0	0
03	57	15	1	1	0	0	0
04	94	18	2	2	1	1	1
05	82	13	2	1	1	1	1
06	59	12	0	0	2	0	0
07	61	12	1	2	0	0	0
08	29	9	0	0	1	1	0
09	36	13	1	1	0	0	0
10	91	16	2	2	1	1	0
11	55	10	0	0	1	0	0
12	58	11	0	1	0	0	0
13	67	14	1	1	0	1	1
14	77	14	1	2	2	1	0
15	71	12	0	0	2	1	0
16	83	16	2	2	1	0	1
17	96	15	2	2	2	0	1
18	87	12	1	1	0	0	1
19	62	11	0	0	0	0	0
20	52	9	0	1	2	1	0
21	46	10	1	0	0	1	0
22	91	20	2	2	1	0	0
23	85	17	2	1	1	1	1
24	48	11	1	1	2	0	0
25	81	17	1	1	1	1	1
26	74	16	2	1	2	1	0
27	68	12	2	1	1	1	1
28	63	12	1	0	0	0	1
29	72	14	0	2	0	0	0
30	99	19	1	1	1	0	0
31	64	13	1	1	0	0	0
32	77	13	1	0	1	1	1
33	88	16	2	2	0	1	0
34	54	09	0	1	1	0	0
35	86	17	1	2	1	0	1
36	73	15	1	1	0	1	0
37	79	15	2	1	0	0	1
38	85	14	2	1	2	1	1
39	96	16	0	1	1	0	1
40	59	12	1	0	0	1	0
41	84	14	1	0	1	0	1
42	71	15	2	1	1	0	0
43	89	15	0	1	0	1	1
44	38	12	1	0	1	1	0
45	62	11	1	1	2	0	1
46	93	16	1	0	1	0	1
47	71	13	2	1	1	0	0
48	55	11	0	1	0	0	0
49	74	15	1	2	0	1	0
50	88	18	1	1	0	1	0

Figure 2.2   Data for the Wintergreen Study

CODING MISSING DATA

Missing data are common in research and evaluation projects. Frequently, a respondent will decline to answer a question for one reason or another (the respondent may consider the question to be nonapplicable or none of the researcher's business, or the respondent may have some other reason for not answering the question). When there are missing data, it is good practice to assign some out-of-range value that can be used as a placeholder in the dataset. In the Wintergreen study, for example, the answer to the question about student motivation could only be "0," "1," or "2." If someone did not answer this question, then a good value to use as a placeholder in the dataset would be "9." Later, when using SPSS to analyze these data, the number "9" would be declared as a *missing value* for this question. Having such a placeholder ensures that the column format for the data remains intact and that the variable truly had missing data rather than simply being skipped over during data entry.

Note that there are no missing data in the Wintergreen study. As an example, however, if the first student had not answered the question regarding motivation, and if "9" were used to represent missing data for this variable, then the record for this student would look like this:

RespondentNumber	aa	pe	sm	ae	r	g	c
01	93	19	9	2	0	0	1

ENTERING DATA

The task of data entry is not usually considered to be a glamorous one. Nevertheless, it is of critical importance, and I encourage anyone who is responsible for data entry to approach the task with the utmost alertness and care. Think about it: You may have just spent a considerable amount of time, effort, and money to collect data upon which you are relying to make an important decision. You may have expended considerable effort to develop a reliable and valid instrument and to ensure a standardized administration of that instrument. You may also have gone to considerable effort to recruit participants for your study. Having gone to such lengths to conduct your study, it is important to preserve the fidelity of your data as you (or your colleague or your assistant) approach the keyboard to enter the data. It is important to keep the data as "clean" (that is, free from data entry error) as possible at every step of the research project.

Data entry can be accomplished in many different ways. We will start with the simple approach of using the "SPSS Data Editor" window. This window opens automatically when you first start SPSS (from the Windows Start button). Using the Data Editor window is simple and straightforward, and works well as long as the person performing the data entry has access to SPSS.

If the person doing the data entry does not have access to SPSS, then they may use a word processing, spreadsheet, or database program to enter the data. This is also an appropriate way to enter data (and even write SPSS programs) in situations where individuals have been asked to minimize their time running SPSS. For example, if your computer is part of a network and SPSS is available only to a limited number of persons at a time, it is more polite and more productive to perform data entry and write programs using some other software and then run SPSS to perform the analyses than it is to tie up the SPSS program so that no one else may use it. This is also a method of allowing you to work on one computer that may not have SPSS and then take your work to another computer that does, when you are ready to perform the analyses.

A couple of notes are important here. If you use a word processor for entering data or writing programs, make sure to choose the option that allows you to save it in text (ASCII) format, so that the many special characters that are associated with a word processing document (such as the unseen formatting commands embedded in a document) are not included in the file. In addition, when using a word processing program, it is far easier to look at raw data as they are being entered or to write SPSS programs when using a fixed font (such as Courier) rather than a proportional font (such as Times New Roman).

Ultimately, data entry is a very important part of the research process. It must be done carefully and attentively. Whether using SPSS or some other program, careful data entry will reduce the amount of time needed to clean the data once analyses have begun. For example, what if the Wintergreen data are being analyzed and you encounter someone whose level of motivation was coded as "4"? Clearly, this out-of-range value would need to be found in the dataset and corrected, and then the analyses would need to be rerun. If much data cleaning must be done, then considerable time may be detracted from the analysis task.

CHAPTER 3

Running SPSS

Chapter Purpose

This chapter introduces fundamental concepts of data entry and running SPSS.

Chapter Goal

To provide readers an opportunity to enter data, run SPSS, and review results.

Chapter Glossary

Chart Editor: SPSS window in which charts can be edited.

Data Editor: SPSS window in which data can be entered and defined.

Designated Window: If multiple windows of one type are opened (e.g., Viewer windows), the one which is active and in which work can be done.

SPSS-Format Data File: A data file saved by SPSS with both data and file definitions.

String: A variable that can have either numbers or letters for values.

Syntax Editor: SPSS window in which command syntax can be written and edited.

Syntax File: File containing SPSS command syntax.

Viewer: SPSS window in which output is displayed.

N ow for the fun we have been waiting for. First, we will take a look at the way SPSS runs and some of the files that it uses. Next, we will create a dataset using the Wintergreen data. Once the data have been entered, we will use the SPSS pull-down menus to conduct the first analyses of these data. We will then use SPSS to draw a chart display-ing the results of one of the analyses. By the end of the chapter, you will have taken the first steps to becoming a proficient SPSS user, and the groundwork will have been prepared to support further investigation into intermediate SPSS topics. Remember, the information that is covered will be easier to understand if you practice at your computer at the same time that you read this book.

You can run SPSS using either the pull-down menus or the Syntax Editor. The former method is a menu-driven approach, while the latter method involves writing your own SPSS programs. We will begin by using the pull-down menus to run SPSS. The use of the syntax window to run SPSS will be deferred until Chapter 7.

SPSS FILES

SPSS uses several types of files. First, there is the file that contains the data that have been entered using the SPSS Data Editor window. This is called, simply enough, the *data file*. Since this file has been saved using SPSS, it is known as an *SPSS-format data file*, and it contains both the data and all the related file definitions (for example, the columns the variables are in, the variable and value labels, and the codes that have been used to define missing values). In contrast, a data file that has been created with your favorite word processor and saved in text format is known as a *raw data file*, and SPSS has to be told how the file has been defined in order to be able to read it.

Once SPSS has conducted an analysis, it displays the results in the output "Viewer" window. The important thing to remember is that you create the data file and instruct SPSS what analysis to perform. SPSS then conducts the analysis and displays the results. The con-tents of this window can be saved in a *viewer file*. SPSS also creates a *journal file* that records the commands run during an SPSS session (this file is not automatically displayed, and we will not be concerned about it at this time).

You have the freedom to call your files whatever you wish, within the restrictions posed by the computer's operating system. Files have a filename followed by a three-character extension (readers unfamiliar with Windows will benefit from a review of any book that discusses file names and directory structure). SPSS has the default convention of naming data files with a *.sav* extension and Viewer files with a *.spo* extension. It is helpful to use the same name for files related to one program and to vary the file extensions to identify the different types of files. For example, in the Wintergreen study, it would make a great deal of sense to name the two files as follows:

```
Data file:        wintergreen.sav
Viewer document:  wintergreen.spo
```

Notice how this approach allows you to keep all the related files in one group, but to easily distinguish each one. Later, if you created an SPSS syntax file to analyze these data, that file could be named using the default *.sps* extension:

```
Syntax file: wintergreen.sps
```

Similarly, if the Wintergreen data were first entered into an external raw data file (to be read by SPSS at a later time), then that file could be named

```
External data file: wintergreen.txt
```

GETTING STARTED: ENTERING THE WINTERGREEN DATA

Let's get started! Launch SPSS from the Windows Start button (that is, click the Start button, select Programs, and select SPSS 12.0 for Windows). At the top of your screen, you will see the pull-down menus, and just below them, you will see a toolbar with several icons. If you place the mouse pointer on any one of the toolbar icons, SPSS will display a label telling you what that icon does. SPSS automatically opens the Data Editor window, and your screen looks like Figure 3.1.

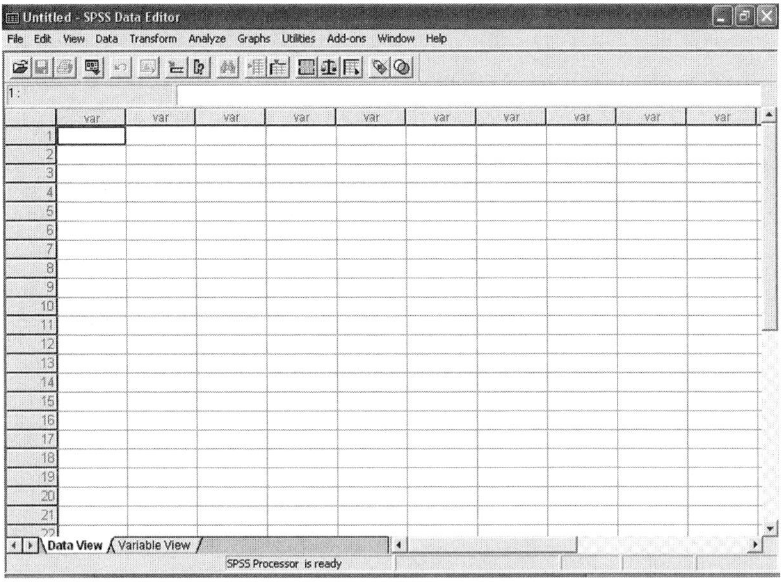

Figure 3.1   SPSS Data Editor Window: Data View

Notice that the Data Editor window looks much like a spreadsheet, in that it is made up of cells defined by both rows and columns (here is where the resemblance ends, however, as the Data Editor is not capable of spreadsheet functions). In the Data Editor window, each row always represents a single record, and each column always represents a single variable. By using the keyboard arrow keys (up, down, right, and left) or your mouse, you can move the cursor around to different cells in the window.

Notice that at this point, each column of data has automatically been called "VAR" by SPSS. Once data have been entered, the first column will be called "VAR00001," the second will be called "VAR00002," and so on. However, this is not very informative, so it is helpful to give the variables more descriptive names. In addition, since it is easier to work with variables if they have short names (and in earlier versions, the variable name was limited to eight characters in length), it too may be less descriptive than we would like, so we will assign a label to the variable name. We will want to assign labels to coded values for the same reason. This idea of labeling the variables and their values is an important one, as it will make data entry easier if you apply the labels before entering the data. In addition, your SPSS output will be much easier to read if the variables and values have been labeled.

To label the first variable, click on the "Variable View" tab at the bottom of the screen, so that your screen now looks like Figure 3.2.

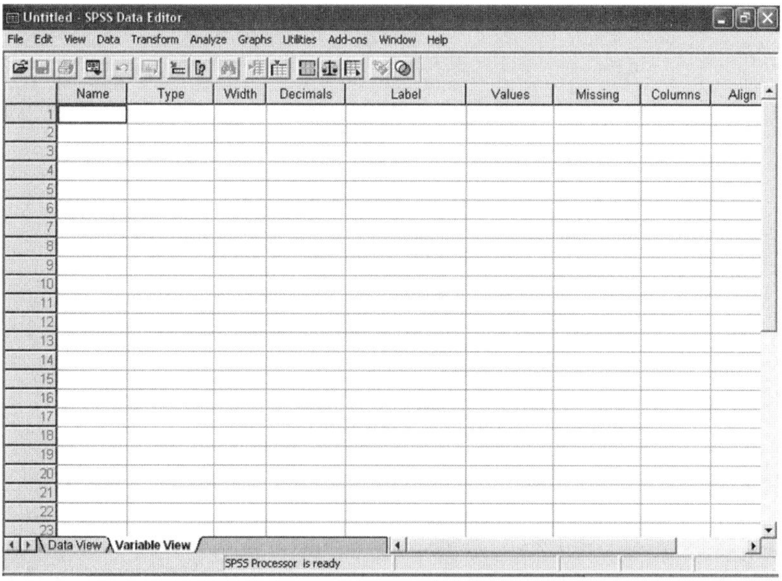

Figure 3.2   SPSS Data Editor Window: Variable View

To label the first variable, place the cursor on the upper-left-hand cell and enter the variable name. Since we will be entering the data from the Wintergreen study, enter "RespondentNumber" in this cell (remember, SPSS does not allow a space in the variable name, so that

"Respondent Number" would not be accepted as a variable name). Now, press the Enter key and notice that SPSS prompts you for additional information about the variable by presenting the screen shown in Figure 3.3.

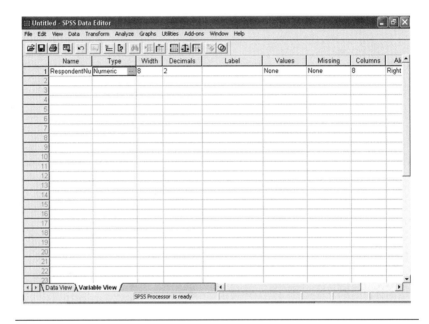

Figure 3.3   SPSS Data Editor Window With First Variable Named

Use your mouse to click on the cell on the same row that is in the "Label" column and enter "Respondent Number" as the variable name. Notice that when you click the "Data View" tab at the bottom of the screen, the first variable is now labeled "RespondentNumber" rather than "VAR."

Now, on the second line, enter "aa" as the variable name for the second variable and "Academic Ability" as the variable name. At this point, notice that you have other options available to you in the Variable View screen. For example, if you click on the ellipsis (". . .") in the **Type** cell, you will be presented with the dialog box shown in Figure 3.4 and several different data types to choose from.

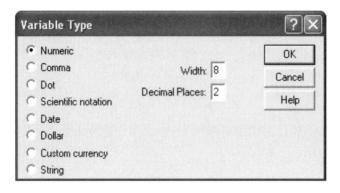

Figure 3.4   Variable Type Dialog Box

By default, the variable is considered to be a number that has up to eight digits. You can tell SPSS to expect a larger number by entering a different size in the **Width** and **Decimal Places** boxes, although that is certainly not necessary for the Wintergreen data. It is important to notice, though, that this is where you can tell SPSS to expect a "String" variable (that is, an alphanumeric variable that can be coded with either numbers or letters) if appropriate. For example, if for the "Gender" variable, we had used "M" instead of "0" for "Male" (and "F" instead of "1" for "Female"), then the Data Editor would not let you enter these values until you told it to expect "Gender" as a "String" variable. You may also choose from several other variable types, as appropriate for your data.

Now, on the third line, enter "pe" as the variable name for the third variable and "Parent Education" as the variable name, and enter "sm" as the variable name for the fourth variable and "Student Motivation" as the variable name. Click on the cell in the fourth row under the column labeled "Values" and then click on the ellipsis that appears in this cell. You will then see the **Value Labels** dialog box shown in Figure 3.5.

Use the Tab key (or the mouse) to bring the cursor to the **Value** box in the **Value Labels** section. Enter a "0" (which is our first value), then tab or click down to the **Value Labels** box and enter "Not willing," and, finally, click the **Add** button. Repeat for the other two values of this variable (refer to the codebook in Figure 2.1 for the values). The Value Labels dialog box will now look like Figure 3.6.

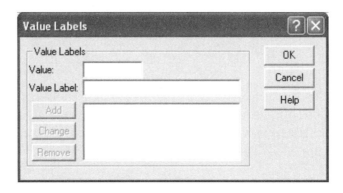

Figure 3.5   Value Labels Dialog Box

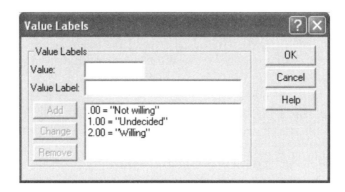

Figure 3.6   Value Labels Dialog Box With Labels Entered

Once you have finished assigning value labels for the student motivation variable, click the **OK** button to return to the Data Editor window.
If you discover later on that for some reason, you need to further define
this variable (for example, if you want to change the labels), you can
always return to this dialog box. As their names suggest, the **Change**
button can be used to change a value label, the **Remove** button can be
used to remove a value label, the **Cancel** button can be used to cancel
your labeling work, and the **Help** button can be used to access the SPSS
help file.

Another important option that is available to you in the "Variable
View" screen is that of declaring the placeholders that have been

used for missing values. For example, remember that "Student Motivation" may take only the values of "0," "1," and "2." Earlier, I suggested that if the measure of student motivation was not available for a respondent, then an out-of-range value such as "9" could be used to indicate that this respondent had missing data. If this has been done, it will be necessary to declare "9" as a missing value by clicking on the ellipsis in the **Missing Values** cell, selecting **Discrete Missing Values** in the Missing Values dialog box that appears, entering "9" as the missing value, and clicking the **OK** button. If, in this case, "9" is not declared as a missing value, then it will be considered to be a non-missing value and treated as such in the data analysis (this, of course, would lead to incorrect results). The Missing Values dialog box now looks like Figure 3.7.

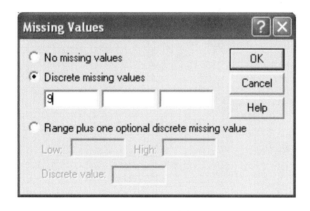

Figure 3.7   Missing Values Dialog Box With Discrete Value Entered

Now go ahead and assign the variable and value labels to the remaining variables (see the codebook in Figure 2.1 for the labels).

To enter the data for the Wintergreen study, return to the Data View screen (by clicking the Data View tab at the bottom of the screen) and move the cursor to the upper-left-hand corner of the screen. Enter "1" for the first respondent number, then move the cursor one cell to the right and enter "93" for the academic ability score, then move the cursor one cell to the right and enter "19" for parent education, and so on. Once all the data for that record are entered, move the cursor to the left-most cell in the second line. You are now ready to enter the second record, and the Data Editor window looks like Figure 3.8.

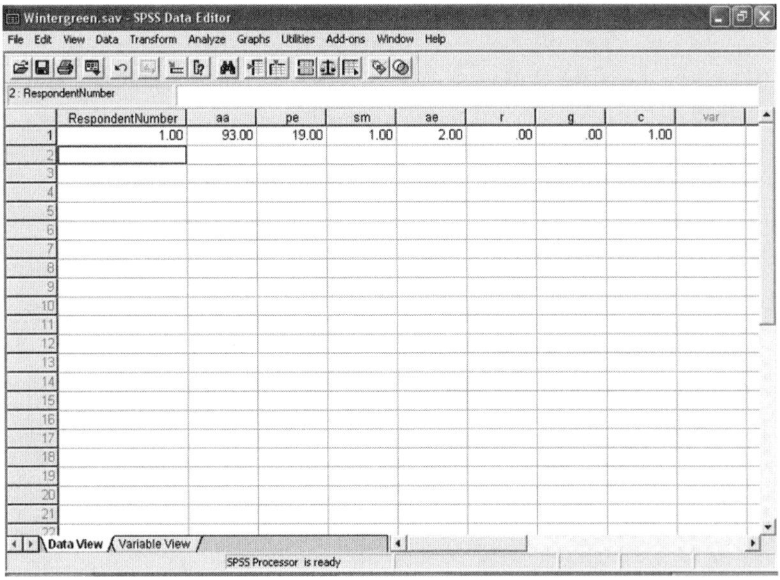

Figure 3.8   Data Editor Window With First Case Entered

Go ahead and enter the first 10 records (see Table 2.2 for the data). Now save the data. This can be done in one of two ways. The first method is to use the **File** pull-down menu and the **Save** choice. Since these data have not previously been saved, you will see a dialog box prompting you to enter a file name. Notice that SPSS provided the default data file extension *(.sav)*. Type in the name "wintergreen" and click the **Save** button. SPSS will then save the data to this file (in general, SPSS will automatically attach the default file extension if you do not type it in, e.g., *.sav* for a data file, *.spo* for an SPSS Viewer file, *.sps* for a syntax file, etc.). As an alternative to using the pull-down menu, you could click on the **Save File** icon in the toolbar (it is the second icon from the left and looks like a diskette). One other alternative would be to select **File Save As . . .** if the dataset had already been saved once but you now want to save it as a new file with a new name.

Go ahead and enter the rest of the Wintergreen data. As a precaution, save your data each time you have entered another 10 records. Once all the data are entered, it is also a good idea to copy the dataset to a diskette (or some other storage device such as a CD or thumb drive) as a backup procedure. Making a backup copy of your work takes far less time than would be required to reenter the data should they accidentally be deleted from your computer.

DATA ANALYSIS

Now you are ready to conduct data analysis with SPSS. First, let's answer the question, "What are the smallest, largest, and average values for Academic Ability and Parent Education?" From the **Analyze** pull-down menu, select **Descriptive Statistics**, then **Descriptives . . .** You will be presented with the dialog box shown in Figure 3.9.

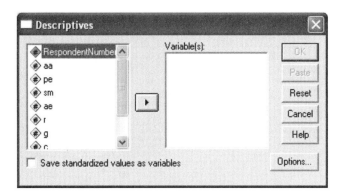

Figure 3.9   Descriptives Dialog Box

This dialog box is typical of what you will see for each of the different analyses SPSS is capable of performing. Click the variable "aa" to select it for analysis, and then click the button with the picture of the right arrow. This will move the variable "aa" from the list of all available variables on the left to the list of selected variables on the right. Now click the variable "pe" in the list on the left, and then click the button with the picture of the right arrow. Next, click the **Options** button to see the "**Descriptives: Options**" dialog box and make sure that there is a "✓" in the boxes for the mean, standard deviation, minimum, and maximum (if a box is empty, then click on it to select it; similarly, if a box is marked, then click on it to deselect it). Then click the **Continue** button.

Now you can select one of the buttons on the right of the **Descriptives** dialog box. If you select **OK**, the analysis will be performed. If you select **Paste**, the SPSS code for this analysis will be written to the syntax window. This is a very important point that we will return to in Chapter 7. If you click **Reset,** the variables you have selected for analysis will be returned to the list of variables on the left (that is, all the available variables will be listed, and none will be selected for analysis). If you select **Cancel,** no analysis will be done and you will return to the window you were in before you chose the **Analyze** pull-down menu (e.g., the Data Editor window). Finally, if you choose **Help**, you will access the SPSS help facility.

At this point, click the **OK** button and run the analysis. SPSS will switch to the SPSS Viewer window and perform the analysis. You will see the following results in this window as shown in Figure 3.10.

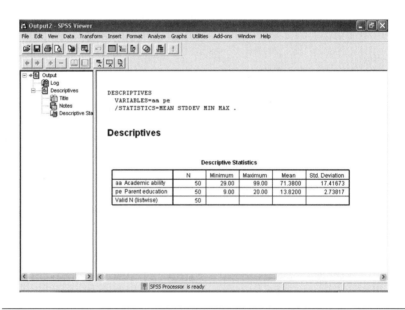

Figure 3.10 Viewer Window With Results From Descriptives Procedure

Congratulations! You are now a beginning SPSS user, and you have just completed a data analysis task using SPSS. Wasn't that considerably easier than performing these analyses by hand? Imagine the increased relative ease if you had 500, 5,000, or 500,000 cases instead of just 50.

Let's take a careful look at the SPSS Viewer window. First, note that the window is divided into two panes. The pane on the left shows the contents of the SPSS output in outline form. In our present example, the first level of the outline is called "Output." Following the Output is the "Log," which contains the commands that SPSS executed to run the analysis. Don't worry if you do not see the log in your output, as that simply means that the option to display the log in the SPSS Viewer has not been selected for your program (however, you may change that option if you wish). Next is the heading for the results of our first analysis, which is labeled "Descriptives." Within the descriptive analysis is a "Title," "Notes (which have been hidden)," and the "Descriptive Statistics" themselves. The contents of any level of this outline can be displayed or hidden by using the **Show** and **Hide** toolbar icons (the fifth and sixth icons on the second row of the toolbars) or by double-clicking on the symbol on that level of the outline.

The pane on the right provides the detailed results of the SPSS analysis. By clicking on any line of the outline on the left, the corresponding detail appears on the right. For example, if you click on "Titles" in the outline on the left, an arrow points to the title line on the right. This is the title that SPSS has provided to the output from the descriptive statistics analysis. You can edit the title by double-clicking on it and then making the changes you wish. If you then click on "Descriptive Statistics" in the outline on the left, an arrow points to the table on the right, which contains the results of the analysis. Thus, by using the outline on the left, you can easily navigate through the output to see the portion in which you are interested. This is particularly helpful when the output is lengthy, in that it is easy to go directly to any portion of the output without having to scroll through the entire output searching for the portion that you want.

Now let's take a look at the results of the analysis. In the first column of the results, SPSS informs us which variables have been analyzed. In the next column, we see the number of cases that were used in the analysis (since there were no missing data for either variable, all 50 cases have been used in the analyses). Next, we see the minimum and maximum values of the variables (for example, the fewest number of years of parent education is 9, while the most is 20). We then see the means and standard deviations for each variable (the mean number of years for parent education was 13.82, with a standard deviation of 2.74). The last line of the output shows the "Valid N (listwise)." This is the number of valid cases (i.e., cases with no missing data). By default,

"Descriptive" will include the total number of valid cases available for any one variable. For example, if there had been no missing cases for the academic ability variable and one missing case for the parent education variable, then 50 cases would have been included in the first analysis, 49 cases would have been included in the second analysis, and 49 cases would have been counted in the "Valid N (listwise)."

It is worth noting that had we not taken the time to assign names and labels to the variables, then instead of seeing "Academic Ability" and "Parent Education" in the left column, we would instead see "aa" and "pe" or "VAR00002" and "VAR00003" (that is, either the variable name without a label or the default name for the variables in the second and third columns of the Data Editor window if they are not given a name). This might be okay for this first analysis, but if you do several analyses with different data and different variables and you do not name and label your variables, you will soon be looking at several different outputs, all with the default variable names. Clearly, this would quickly become confusing. In addition, you may wish to show this output to someone who is not familiar with the study or the dataset, and it is helpful for the person to be presented with variable labels. In short, make it easy on yourself and others by using variable and value labels.

Go ahead and save the output. From the **File** pull-down menu, select **Save**. Give the output file a name such as "Wintergreen.spo" (since this is the output from the first analysis of the Wintergreen data), and click the **Save** button. Notice that you can use standard Windows procedures to select the drive or directory in which to save the file (readers unfamiliar with Windows procedures will benefit from a review of any book in which they are covered).

If you wish to switch between the Data Editor window and the Viewer window, you may do so by choosing from the open windows, which are listed in the **Window** pull-down menu. Alternatively, you can click on the buttons on the Windows task bar at the bottom of your screen. In general, you can use either of these techniques to switch among any of the windows that are currently open.

Now let's obtain frequency distributions to answer the question, "What are the demographic characteristics of the students in the Wintergreen study, how motivated were they, and how likely to succeed in college were they rated?" From the **Analyze** pull-down menu, select **Descriptive Statistics**, and then select **Frequencies . . .** You will see the dialog box Shown in Figure 3.11.

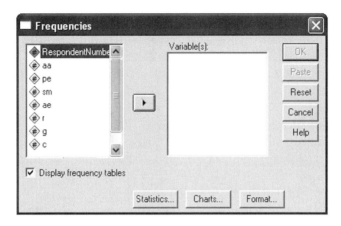

Figure 3.11 Frequencies Dialog Box

Click on "sm" in the list of variables available for analysis on the left. Then click the button with the picture of the right-hand arrow. The selected variable will be moved to the list on the right. Repeat this procedure to select the variables "ae," "r," "g," and "c." If you wish, you could also select "aa" or "pe," but this is not a particularly meaningful way to summarize the data for those variables. Similarly, you could also select "RespondentNumber," but you already know that you will get a list of values from 1 to 50, each with one case (if you do not see what I mean, I encourage you to select "RespondentNumber" to include in this analysis, and then study the output). You will notice that you have several options available in this dialog box, but we will not select any of them at this time. Go ahead and click the **OK** button. Once SPSS has completed the analysis, the results appear in the Viewer window.

First, note that on the left-hand side of the window, the outline for the results of the Frequencies analysis has been added below the outline for the Descriptives analysis (of course, if you opened and designated a new Viewer window, or if you ended your SPSS session after the Descriptives analysis and started a new session before conducting the Frequencies analysis, then the contents of the Viewer window would contain only the results of the Frequencies analysis). Reading down this outline, you first see "Frequencies" as a second-level heading in the outline, and beneath this heading are headings for the "Title," "Notes," "Statistics," and then the "Frequency Tables" as a third-level heading, which includes as a fourth-level heading the results for "Student Motivation," "Advisor Evaluation," "Religious Affiliation," "Gender," and "Community Type." By clicking on any one of these fourth-level headings in the outline, you see the corresponding results of the analysis in the right-hand side of the window.

You will see that the default title SPSS has provided for this set of analyses is simply the word "Frequencies." Again, you may double-click on the title to edit it if you wish. The "Statistics" table details the number of valid and missing cases for each variable that has been included in the analysis.

In the left-hand pane of the window, click on "Student Motivation" to see the results for the frequencies analysis for that variable as shown in Figure 3.12.

sm Student Motivation

		Frequency	Percent	Valid percent	Cumulative percent
Valid	.00 Not willing	13	26.0	26.0	26.0
	1.00 Undecided	23	46.0	46.0	72.0
	2.00 Willing	14	28.0	28.0	100.0
	Total	50	100.0	100.0	

Figure 3.12   Partial Results From Frequencies Procedure

These results include the frequency of cases that responded with each value of the variable, followed by the percentage of cases, the valid percentage of cases, and the cumulative percentage of cases. Thus, in the "Frequency" column, we see that 13 students indicated that they were "Not willing" to spend extra hours studying, 23 students were "Undecided," and 14 students were "Willing" to spend extra hours studying. Next, there are three columns of percentages. The "Percent" column is the percentage of students in each category, based on the total number of cases. If there were cases with missing data, then there would be a fourth row for this variable (labeled

"Missing") and the percentage of cases in the "Missing" category would also be calculated. The next column, labeled "Valid Percent," shows the percentage of cases in each category based on the number of cases with non-missing data. For example, if two cases had missing data, then these two cases would be excluded from the analysis and the percentage in each category of student motivation would be based on 48 cases. Because no cases in this example have missing data, the two columns ("Percent" and "Valid Percent") show identical results. The fourth column shows the cumulative percentage for the frequency distribution.

The rest of the output is similar in format and shows the results for the other variables. You should see that 26% of the students were evaluated as "Likely to fail" in college, 50% were evaluated as "Could succeed or could fail," and 24% were evaluated as "Likely to succeed." Among the students, 42% indicated that they were Catholic, 40% indicated that they were Protestant, and 18% indicated that they were Jewish. In terms of gender, 56% of the students were male, and 44% were female. Finally, 60% of the students came from an urban community, while 40% came from a rural community.

DRAWING CHARTS

You can draw charts using the SPSS chart feature. Charts are very important for displaying data, whether for the purpose of examining the data or for communicating the results of an analysis. To draw a chart, simply select this option (if it is available) when conducting an analysis. Let's look at an example. First, return to the **Frequencies** dialog box, select only the variable "sm" (you can deselect variables by clicking on them and then clicking the button with the left-hand arrow on it), and then click on the **Charts . . .** button. You will see the dialog box shown in Figure 3.13.

Select **Bar Chart** as the chart type and **Percentages** as the chart values. Then click the **Continue** button to return to the previous dialog box. Finally, click the **OK** button to run the analysis. SPSS first creates the frequency distribution and then draws the chart. You can see the chart by clicking on "Bar Chart" in the outline on the left-hand side of the Viewer window. It should look something like Figure 3.14 (depending on how your *Preferences* are set).

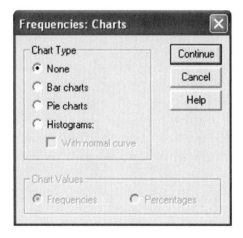

Figure 3.13 Frequencies Chart Dialog Box

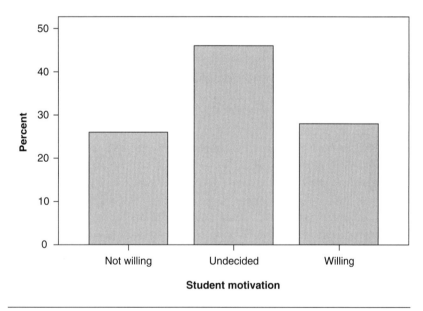

Figure 3.14 Chart Drawn With Default Specifications

Double-click the chart to enter the "Chart Editor" window. There are many things you can do with your chart once you are in this window.

For example, I would like to change the scale of the Y-axis so that the percentages are displayed in a range from 0 to 100 (I encourage you to display the full range whenever you are using percentages as an axis scale unless you have a particular reason to do otherwise). From the **Edit** pull-down menu, choose **Select Y Axis**, and then click the **Scale** tab in the properties dialog box. Click the box for the "Maximum" under the "Auto" column so that it does not have a check mark in it, and then change the "50" to "100" in the box under the "Custom" column. The dialog box will now look Figure 3.15.

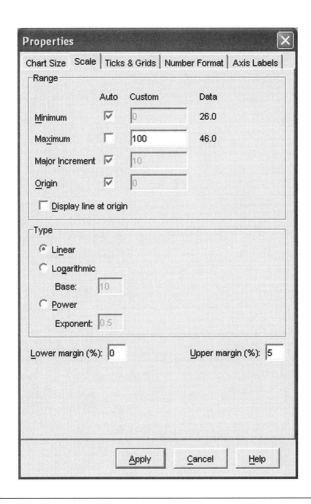

Figure 3.15 Chart Properties Dialog Box

Now click the **Apply** button, and notice that the chart has been rescaled. If you wish to apply similar formatting to other charts, then you can save these changes as a chart template. To do so, in the Chart Editor window, from the **File** pull-down menu, select **Save Chart Template**. You will then be asked to specify the features of the template you wish to save, and then after clicking the **Continue** button, you will be asked to specify a name and location for the template to be saved. You can then apply this template to charts that you draw at a later time. To see how this works, save the chart template as "MyFrequencies" (SPSS gives the chart template the default extension of *.sgt*), run the Frequencies procedure for another variable (for example, "Community Type") and then double-click the chart to open the Chart Editor window. Next, from the **File** pull-down menu, select **Apply Chart Template . . .** select the template named "MyFrequencies.sgt," and click the **Open** button to apply to template to the new chart.

Now close the Chart Editor window and return to the Viewer window.

DESIGNATING A WINDOW

SPSS allows you to have more than one output window open at a time. To open a second (or third, or fourth, etc.) window, from the **File** pull-down menu, select **New,** and then **Output.** Since SPSS can work with only one active data file at a time, if you choose **File, New, Data,** it will want to close the current data file and open a new one.

Although you can have more than one Viewer window open at a time, only one of them can be *designated.* In other words, you may have more than one Viewer window open at a time, but when you click the **OK** button from a dialog box, SPSS can display only the results of an analysis in one of the open Viewer windows. How does SPSS know which one to use? It uses the one that has been designated. You can tell which window has been designated by looking at the center of the bottom of the screen. If there is a red exclamation point there, then the window has been designated. If no exclamation point appears at the bottom of the window, then that window has not been designated. To change which window is designated, simply click the icon with the exclamation point that appears at the right end of the upper toolbar in the Viewer window.

Having more than one window open affords you options that you otherwise would not have. As a simple example, consider the two analyses we have done so far. You may want the results of the analysis of the academic ability and parent education data to be saved in one Viewer file and the results of the frequency distributions of the other variables to be saved in a different file. In this case, you would send the results to two different Viewer windows by designating the first window and running the first analysis, and then designating the second window and running the second analysis. You could then save the results in two different files. The more you use SPSS, the more you will encounter different scenarios and reasons for which you will wish to exercise the option of using different output windows. (Note: The concept of having multiple open windows and changing which one is designated also applies to syntax windows, which are discussed in Chapter 7.)

EXERCISE ONE

At the end of a semester-long course, a teacher decides to obtain students' feedback regarding their perceptions of the course through the administration of an anonymous survey. The fourth item on the survey states, "I liked the text that was used in this course," and students are asked whether they "Agree," are "Undecided," or "Disagree" with this statement. All 10 students complete the survey, and the following hypothetical data are collected:

	Student
Number	Item_04
01	Agree
02	Agree
03	Undecided
04	Agree
05	Agree
06	Undecided
07	Agree
08	Agree
09	Agree
10	Agree

(Continued)

Use SPSS to analyze these data to answer the question, "Did students in the course like the text that was used?" You will need to create a codebook, code the data (use "1" to indicate "Agree," "2" to indicate "Undecided," and "3" to indicate "Disagree"), enter the data, assign variable names and labels, assign value labels, generate a frequency distribution for this item, and state the answer to the research question.

CHAPTER 4

Data Manipulation

Chapter Purpose

This chapter introduces fundamental concepts of working with data.

Chapter Goal

To provide readers with skills to change the coding scheme of a dataset, compute data values, select cases from a dataset, and list cases in the Viewer.

Chapter Glossary

Compute: To create a new variable.

List Cases: To list the values of variables for a number of cases, often done to check that recoded or computed variables have assumed the correct values.

Numeric: A variable that can have only numbers for values.

Recode: To change the values of a variable.

Visual Bander: An SPSS tool to recode values of a variable into groups.

Data frequently need to be manipulated before analyses are conducted. They may need to be recoded, computations may need to be made, new variables may need to be created, or certain records may need to be selected from the dataset. These topics are covered in this chapter.

CHANGING THE CODING SCHEME USING RECODE

There are times when it is necessary to change the coding scheme of the data. One example would be if you wanted to take several values of a variable and divide them into groups. For instance, you may have data on individuals who range from 15 to 25 years of age, but for the purpose of analysis, you are concerned about the difference between those who are less than 21 and those who are 21 or older. As another example, we may want to group the students in the Wintergreen study by their level of academic ability (using increments of 10 points), so that we can describe the percentage of students who scored in the range "0–9," "10–19," "20–29," and so on.

As a third example, consider the case where you have a measure with 10 items, each scored "1" through "5." However, it may be that 7 of the questions are worded so that a score of "5" is "high," while 3 of the questions are worded so that a score of "1" is "high." If you wanted to get a total score for this measure by adding the answers to all 10 questions, you would first need to recode the 3 reverse-worded items so that a "1" was scored as if it were a "5" (and a "2" was scored as if it were a "4," a "4" as if it were a "2," and a "5" as if it were a "1"). Otherwise, the items would not have a common direction, and it would not make sense to add them to get a summative score.

In all three of these cases, the task is accomplished by *recoding* the data. From the **Transform** pull-down menu, select **Recode**. You now have to choose whether to recode the data **Into Same Variables . . .** or **Into Different Variables . . .** If you choose the former, your original data will be converted into the recoded data and you will no longer be able to conduct analyses on the original data. If you choose the latter, you will create a new variable that has the values of the recoded original data. The option you choose will be based on your analysis plans (that is, whether or not you will need to continue to use the original data).

Let's recode the academic ability data into a new variable. From the **Transform** pull-down menu, select **Recode**, and then select **Into Different Variables . . .** You will be presented with the dialog box shown in Figure 4.1.

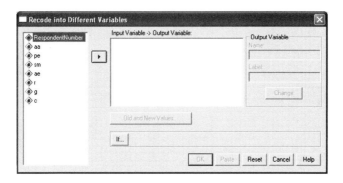

Figure 4.1   Recode Into Different Variables Dialog Box

Select the variable "aa" from the list of available variables on the left, and click the button with the right-hand arrow. Click on the **Output Variable Name** box, and enter a name for the new variable (such as "aa_new"), and then click on the **Output Variable Label** box, and enter a label (such as "Recoded Academic Ability"). Then click the **Change** button. Now click the **Old and New Values . . .** button. You will see the dialog box shown in Figure 4.2.

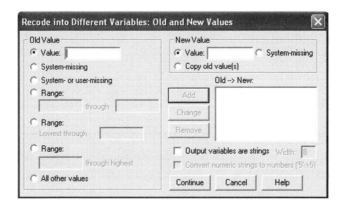

Figure 4.2   Old and New Values Dialog Box

Select **Old Value, Range,** and then enter "0" through "9." Enter "0" for the **New Value.** Then click the **Add** button. Return to the **Range** box, and enter "10" through "19" for the range; return to the

New Value box, enter a "1" for the value, and click the **Add** button. Continue for the remaining groups of ranges (the last one will assign the values "90" through "100" to group number "9"). If you make a mistake along the way, you can correct it by using the **Change** and **Remove** buttons. Once you have completed defining the groups, click the **Continue** button. You will return to the previous dialog box. If you now click the **OK** button, the new variable will be created. If you return to the Data Editor window, you will see that the new variable "aa_new" has been added to the dataset. You can also attach labels or attributes to this variable through the Variable View screen in the Data Editor (click the "Variable View" tab at the bottom of the Data Editor window to see this screen).

Now, from the **Analyze** pull-down menu, select **Descriptive Statistics** and **Frequencies**. You will see "aa_new" is now one of the variables that is available for analysis. Select this variable (and deselect any other variables that may be selected) and click the **OK** button. The results will look like those shown in Figure 4.3.

Recoded Academic Ability

		Frequency	Percent	Valid percent	Cumulative percent
Valid	2.00 20-29	1	2.0	2.0	2.0
	3.00 30-39	2	4.0	4.0	6.0
	4.00 40-49	3	6.0	6.0	12.0
	5.00 50-59	8	16.0	16.0	28.0
	6.00 60-69	7	14.0	14.0	42.0
	7.00 70-79	10	20.0	20.0	62.0
	8.00 80-89	11	22.0	22.0	84.0
	9.00 90-100	8	16.0	16.0	100.0
	Total	50	100.0	100.0	

Figure 4.3   Grouped Frequency Distribution of Academic Ability

If you wish, you can obtain a frequency distribution for the variable "aa" as a comparison. This will help you see the potential descriptive value of this data transformation.

CHANGING THE CODING SCHEME USING VISUAL BANDER

You may also use SPSS's **Visual Bander**, which you may find easier to use, to recode data into groups. From the **Transform** pull-down menu, select **Visual Bander . . .** The first Visual Bander dialog box will appear, as shown in Figure 4.4.

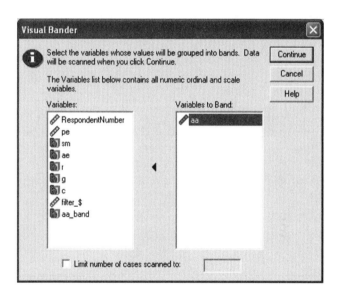

Figure 4.4   First Visual Bander Dialog Box

Click the variable "aa" in the list of "Variables" and the right arrow to move it to the list of "Variables to Band" (notice that SPSS allows use of the Visual Bander only to group variables measured on a *scaled* [interval or ratio] or ordinal level of measurement). Click **Continue** to reach the second Visual Bander dialog box (shown in Figure 4.5), click "aa" to begin banding the variable, and enter "aa_band" as the name in the "Banded Variable" box. The second Visual Bander dialog box now looks like that shown in Figure 4.5.

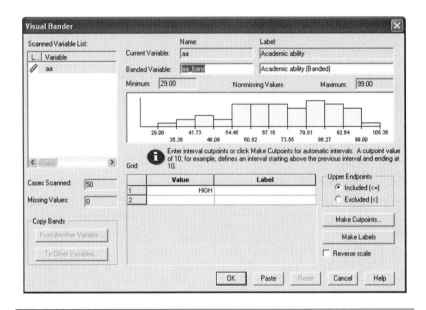

Figure 4.5   Second Visual Bander Dialog Box

Click the **Make Cutpoints** button to reach the third Visual Bander dialog box. Select **Equal Width Intervals** if it is not already selected, enter "9" as the **First Cutpoint Location**, "9" for the **Number of Cutpoints**, and "10" as the **Width** of the cutpoints. The third dialog box will look like Figure 4.6.

Click the **Apply** button, and when prompted that "the existing cutpoint definitions will be replaced," click the **OK** button to return to the second Visual Bander dialog box. Notice that the Visual Bander has created the desired values for the new variable. Now click the **Make Labels** button and the Visual Bander automatically assigns labels to the new values. If you do not like the new values or their labels, simply click on the box you wish to edit. The second dialog box now looks like Figure 4.7.

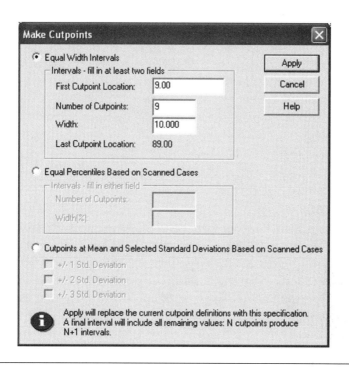

Figure 4.6   Third Visual Bander Dialog Box

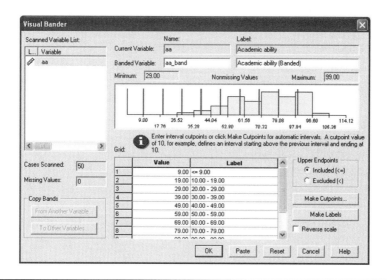

Figure 4.7   Second Visual Bander Dialog Box With Values and Labels Created

Click the **OK** button, and when prompted that "Banding specifications will create 1 variable," click the **OK** button to create the new variable. Look at the Data Editor to see that the new variable has been created (you will see each case's value for the variable if you click the "Data View" tab, and you will see the name, label, and other characteristics of the variable if you click the "Variable View" tab). Finally, use the Frequencies procedure to obtain a frequency distribution for "aa_band," and notice that it produces the same results as seen in Figure 4.3.

COMPUTING DATA VALUES

You may need to do some sort of computation using the data you have collected before conducting an analysis. For example, parent education is a variable in the Wintergreen dataset. This variable is the average number of years of schooling for the student's mother and father. However, during actual data collection, it is unlikely that the student would compute this average for the researcher. Rather, the student would be asked the number of years of schooling each parent had, and the researcher would calculate the average (more precisely, the researcher would have the computer calculate the average).

Imagine that the dataset does not have the parent education variable (named "pe") and instead has two other variables: one for mother's education (which might be named "me" or "mom_ed") and one for father's education (which might be named "de" or "dad_ed"). For the purpose of illustration, return to the Variable View screen in the Data Editor window, move the cursor to the first unoccupied row, create a variable called "mom_ed" by entering that name in the "Name" column, and label the variable "Mother's Education." Then move to the next row, and create a variable called "dad_ed" by entering that name in the "Name" column, and label the variable "Father's Education." Now go to the Data View screen, and enter "18" as the value for "mom_ed" for the first record, "13" as the value for the second record, and "14" as the value for the third record. Then enter "20" as the value for "dad_ed" for the first record, "11" as the value for the second record, and "16" as the value for the third record.

To create the parent education variable, from the **Transform** pull-down menu, select **Compute . . .** Enter "par_ed" in the **Target Variable** box, and in the **Numeric Expression** box, enter the following:

```
(mom_ed + dad_ed) / 2
```

You can do this by either clicking on the variable names, the right arrow, and the number and function pad, or you can type directly into the **Numeric Expression** box. The dialog box will now look like Figure 4.8.

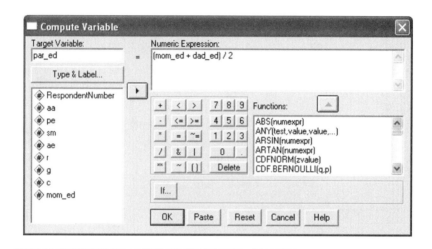

Figure 4.8   Compute Dialog Box

Click the **OK** button to compute the new variable. SPSS will create a new variable called "par_ed," which will appear in the next available right-hand column in the Data View screen and the next available row in the Variable View screen. You will see the computed variable for the three cases for which you entered data.

SELECTING RECORDS FROM A DATASET

Sometimes you want to conduct an analysis based on only certain cases in your dataset. Suppose, for example, you had collected data from students in each grade of a high school, but for a particular question of interest, you wanted to limit your analyses to only those students in 12th grade. As another example, you may decide there is some reason for restricting an analysis of the Wintergreen data to only those students who come from a rural community. To do this, from the **Data** pull-down menu, choose **Select Cases . . .** You will see the Select Cases dialog box shown in Figure 4.9.

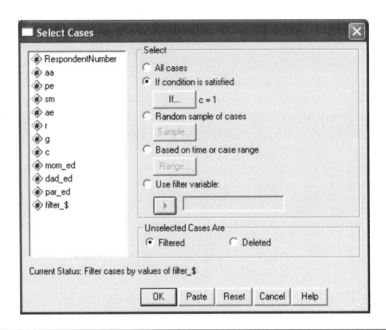

Figure 4.9   Select Cases Dialog Box

Now select **If condition is satisfied**, and then click the **If . . .**
button. Click on the variable "c" from the list on the left, then type " = 1"
(you could also use the function and number pads to enter " = 1"). The
Select Cases: If dialog box will appear as shown in Figure 4.10.

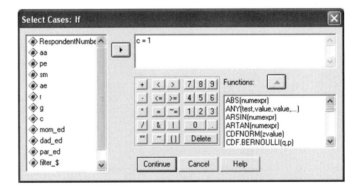

Figure 4.10   Select Cases Dialog Box With Selection Criteria Entered

Click the **Continue** button, and, finally, click the **OK** button to select the cases. When you select cases, you will notice that in the Data Editor window, a slash mark appears through the record number of those cases that were not selected (the selected cases, which remain available for analysis, do not have a slash mark through their record numbers). If you wish to include all of the cases in a later analysis, simply return to the **Select Cases** dialog box, and select **All Cases**.

LISTING CASES

If you have manipulated your data, then it is good practice to first list and study the contents of a few records before conducting your analyses. This will ensure that you have correctly instructed SPSS how to manipulate the data. If you notice any problems, then go back and make any necessary corrections (for example, you may have entered incorrect information in a **Compute** dialog box). This important step takes only a moment, and it will help ensure the accuracy of your analysis.

One method of listing cases is to use the **List Cases** command available through SPSS syntax (syntax is discussed in Chapter 7). Cases may also be listed using the **Summarize Cases** command in the pull-down menus (this command can also be used to compute certain statistics for variables). To list cases using this command, from the **Analyze** pull-down menu, select **Reports**, and then choose **Case Summaries . . .** The following dialog box shown in Figure 4.11 will appear.

Highlight the variables from the list on the left that you wish to list (for example, "mom_ed," "dad_ed," and "par_ed.") Make sure the **Display Cases** option is selected (it will have a check mark in the box next to the option), and in the **Limit cases to first** box, enter some small number (like 5 or 10). Since what we are doing at this point is making sure that you have instructed SPSS to correctly perform a computation, it is necessary to list only the first few cases. If the first few cases are correct, then the remaining cases will also be correct. In addition, if the dataset has a large number of records, computer processing time will be wasted, as will time spent editing the output. Then click the **OK** button to run this procedure. The output from this command is shown in Figure 4.12.

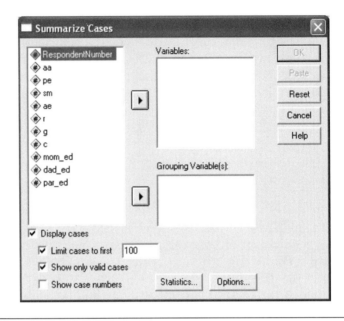

Figure 4.11 Summarize Cases Dialog Box

Summarize

Case Processing Summary[a]

	Cases					
	Included		Excluded		Total	
	N	Percent	N	Percent	N	Percent
mom_ed Mother's education	3	60.0%	2	40.0%	5	100.0%
dad_ed	3	60.0%	2	40.0%	5	100.0%
par_ed	3	60.0%	2	40.0%	5	100.0%

a. Limited to first 5 cases

Figure 4.12 (Continued)

Case Summaries[a]

		mom_ed Mother's education	dad_ed	par_ed
1		18.00	20.00	19.00
2		13.00	11.00	12.00
3		14.00	16.00	15.00
Total	N	3	3	3

a. Limited to first 5 cases

Figure 4.12   Results From Summarize Procedure

EXERCISE TWO

Suppose a researcher has collected data regarding subjects' age, but the data analysis plan calls for making comparisons between subjects who are 18 years of age or less and subjects who are older than 18 years of age. Using the following hypothetical data, create a new variable called "AgeGroup" and assign this variable a value of "1" for the younger subjects and a value of "2" for the older subjects (be sure to label all variables and the values of the new variable). List the data to confirm that the new variable was coded correctly.

Student	
Number	Age
01	17
02	21
03	18
04	23
05	16
06	22
07	17
08	18
09	21
10	19

EXERCISE THREE

Suppose a teacher gives three tests during a semester, and at the end of the semester would like to obtain an average score for each student. Using the following hypothetical data, create a new variable whose value is the average score for each student. List the data to confirm that the new variable was coded correctly.

	Student		
Number	Test 1	Test 2	Test 3
01	90	85	95
02	85	85	85
03	90	80	70
04	70	80	75
05	75	85	80

CHAPTER 5

Managing Data Files

Chapter Purpose

This chapter introduces fundamental concepts of working with data files.

Chapter Goal

To provide readers with skills to read data files created with other software, and to merge data files by either adding cases or adding variables.

Chapter Glossary

Adding Cases: Merging two or more data files so that each file contributes cases, but not variables, to the new data file.

Adding Variables: Merging two or more data files so that each file contributes variables to the new data file.

Key Variable: When adding variables, the variable on which the files are sorted to ensure that data from each file, for a given record, end up properly matched.

Text File: Data saved in ASCII format using a word processing or other program.

Earlier in this book, we entered the data from the Wintergreen study using the SPSS Data Editor window. However, there are other ways to enter data, and sometimes you may wish (or need) to enter data using an alternative method. Similarly, someone else may have done the data entry and provided you with the dataset, but the person may not have used

SPSS for the data entry. In this chapter, we will look at two alternatives for getting data: reading data from a *text file* (also known as an ASCII file) and reading data that have been entered using another software package. This chapter will also explore a second topic of importance for managing data files, namely, how to combine two different data files (please note that for learning purposes, the topic of managing data files has been saved until this chapter, although in practice, one typically combines data files before manipulating the data).

READING ASCII DATA

Suppose that you had to enter the Wintergreen data using a computer that did not have SPSS, so that you could analyze them later using a computer that did have SPSS. To do so, you could simply use your favorite word processor. Remember to save your data as a *text file*, so that the special characters that define a *document* are not included in the file. The typical word processing program running in the Windows environment will provide you with an option to save a file as "MS-DOS text" or "Plain Text" with MS-DOS text encoding and "CR/LF" (carriage return/line feed) to end the lines. If you were entering the Wintergreen data as a text file using your word processor, you would probably want to give it a name that was parallel to the other Wintergreen files and yet also unique from them. I would suggest a name such as "Wintergreen.txt."

Let's take another look at the Wintergreen data. If you type the data using this word processing program, keeping a fixed row and column format, they will appear as shown in Figure 5.1.

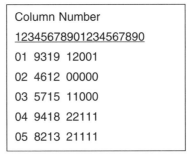

Figure 5.1   Example of Text-Based Data Entry

The respondent number has been entered in columns 1–2, the Academic Ability score has been entered in columns 4–5, Parent Education has been entered in columns 6–7, Student Motivation has been entered in column 9, Advisor Evaluation has been entered in column 10, Religious Affiliation has been entered in column 11, Gender has been entered in column 12, and Community Type has been entered in column 13. Notice that I have skipped columns 3 and 8. This was not necessary (and I could have chosen to skip different columns had I wished), but I elected to have these spaces in the dataset to make the data easier to look at. This can be handy for helping you keep your place when you are doing data entry and there are many variables for each case. For example, imagine that you are entering the data from a survey that has 5 sets of 10 items, for a total of 50 items. You might choose to leave a blank column between each set of items.

You may also notice that all of the numbers line up in each of the columns. This is because I have used a fixed font (in this example, I have used a font called Courier New). If you use a proportional font (for example, Times New Roman), your data will be much harder to see. As I mentioned earlier, this type of data file (in which all the rows and columns line up) is called a *fixed-length flat file.* Go ahead and enter these five cases, and save them in a text file called "Wintergreen.txt."

As an alternative, you may use a form of data entry that does not require the data to line up in columns. This form is known as *freefield format,* and it requires only that variables be recorded in the same order for each case and that they be separated by spaces or commas (that is, a *delimiter*). Readers interested in this format may learn more about it from the SPSS manuals.

Once you have saved this dataset as a text file, you will want to read it with SPSS. From the **File** pull-down menu, select **Read Text Data . . .** to see the **Open File** dialog box. Select the "Wintergreen.txt" data file and click the **Open** button to start the **Text Import Wizard** and view the first of six "Text Import Wizard" steps as shown in Figure 5.2.

Click the **Next** button to go to the second step. Here you will want to note that the variables are aligned in fixed-width columns and that the first row does not contain variable names. The dialog box will look like Figure 5.3.

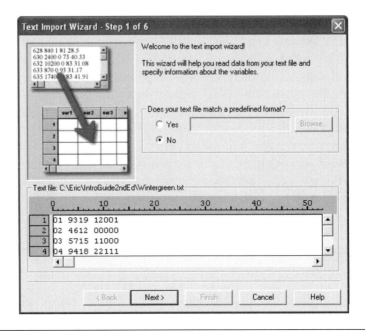

Figure 5.2   Text Import Wizard First Dialog Box

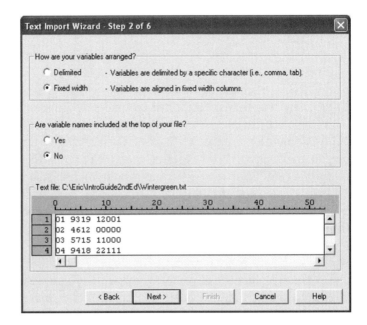

Figure 5.3   Text Import Wizard Second Dialog Box

Click the **Next** button to go to the third step. Note that the data begin on the first line, that each case requires only one line, and that we want to import all the data. The dialog box will look like Figure 5.4.

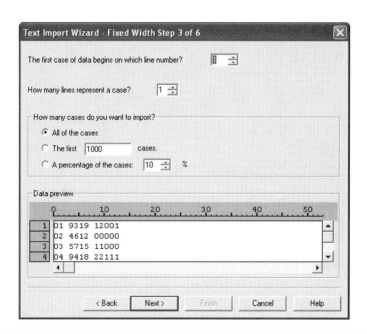

Figure 5.4   Text Import Wizard Third Dialog Box

Click the **Next** button to go to the fourth step. Click in the data view area to insert vertical lines indicating where each variable starts. You may need to refer to the codebook to remind yourself of the column positions for each variable. The dialog box will look like Figure 5.5.

Click on the **Next** button to go to the fifth step. Then click on each variable in the data preview, and then enter the variable name in the dialog box. Figure 5.6 shows the dialog box after the first three variables have been named. Continue the naming process until all the variables have been named.

Click the **Next** button to go to the final step. If you wish, you may save the file format for future use (for example, if you were going to repeat the same survey in the same format on more than one occasion), and you may paste the syntax to the Syntax Editor if you wish. The dialog box will look like Figure 5.7.

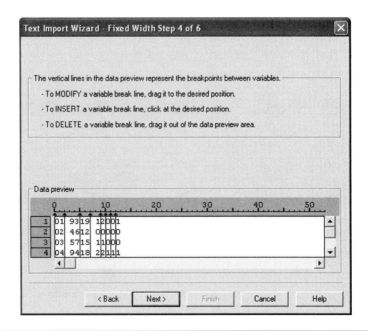

Figure 5.5 Text Import Wizard Fourth Dialog Box

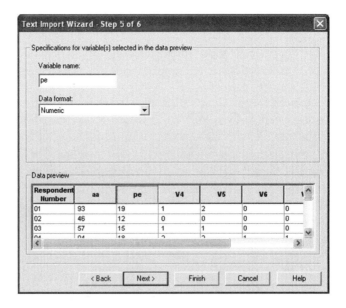

Figure 5.6 Text Import Wizard Fifth Dialog Box With First Three Variables Named

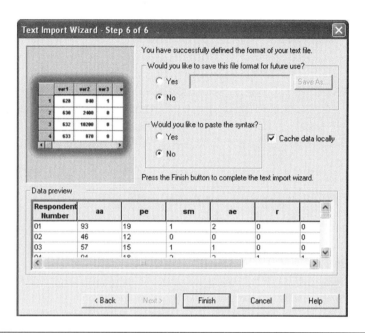

Figure 5.7   Text Import Wizard Sixth Dialog Box

Click the **Finish** button to read the data. Take a look at the Data Editor to confirm that SPSS has read the data from the text file and that they match the first five records of the Wintergreen dataset. At this point, you can save the file, which will be written as an SPSS-format data file.

IMPORTING FILES FROM OTHER SOFTWARE PACKAGES

SPSS is capable of recognizing data that have been entered and saved using other software packages. For example, imagine that the Wintergreen data have been entered using Microsoft Excel. From the **File** pull-down menu, select **Open** and then select **Data . . .** You will see a dialog box allowing you to browse for the file you wish to open. At the bottom of the dialog box is a selection field called "**Files of type:**". From this list you can choose **Excel** *(*.xls).* SPSS will then recognize that it is reading an Excel file. As SPSS is opening the Excel file, it will present you with the **Opening File Options** dialog box. Note that if the first row of the Excel spreadsheet contains the names of the variables rather than data, you will need to select **Read variable names** in this dialog box. Also note that SPSS reads only one sheet at a time from the Excel workbook. If you have multiple sheets in a workbook that are related to one another, SPSS can read them using the Database Wizard (accessed from the **File, Open Database, New Query . . .** pull-down menus). It is also worth noting that many database and spreadsheet software packages can save (or export) data as an ASCII file, and you already know from the previous section how to read such a file.

MERGING DATA FILES: ADDING CASES

Sometimes data for a study are collected at different times, and sometimes they are entered at different times or by different people. In either of these cases, you may need to combine data files. The first method of combining files we will discuss involves adding cases to a file (also known as *appending* files). Imagine that data have been collected for an additional 50 students for the Wintergreen study. These data have been entered and saved as an SPSS data file. We would now like to combine this new file with the original Wintergreen data file, so that we end up with a single data file with 100 cases. To do so, first open the first data file. Next, from the **Data** pull-down window, select **Merge Files**, and then select **Add Cases . . .** The dialog box shown in Figure 5.8 will appear.

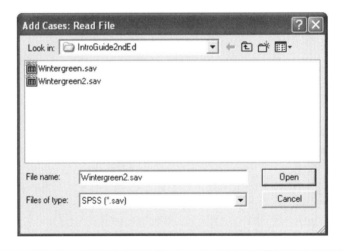

Figure 5.8   Add Cases Dialog Box

Enter the name of the file (in this example, the file name is "Wintergreen2.sav") with the cases to be added, and then click the **Open** button. The dialog box shown in Figure 5.9 will appear.

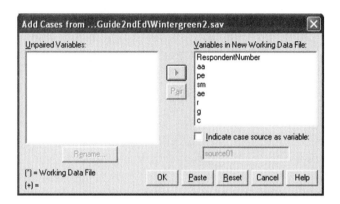

Figure 5.9   Add Cases Dialog Box

Click the **OK** button to add the cases in the second dataset to those in the first. The Data Editor window will now contain the total number of records. You may want to save this new combined file (perhaps giving it a new file name) in order to have a single data file with all the records (and thus be able to skip the step of appending one file to another the next time you want to conduct an analysis using all of the cases). It is also a good idea to list a few cases using the **Case Summaries . . .** command to see that you have correctly instructed SPSS how to merge the data.

MERGING DATA FILES: ADDING VARIABLES

There is another way of combining two data files that occurs when data on additional variables have been collected for the same persons who are already in the study. Imagine, for example, that a new variable is measured for the same 50 students in the Wintergreen study. For example, the new variable could be high school grade point average, and it could be stored in a file called "Wintergreen3.sav" (the variable Respondent Number would also be included in this file). What we would like to do is create a single data file with 50 cases and all of the variables.

First, the data in each file must be saved as an SPSS-format data file. Each file must also be sorted in ascending order by some *key* variable (in this case, the variable RespondentNumber). To sort a file, from the

Data pull-down menu select **Sort Cases** . . . The dialog box shown in Figure 5.10 will appear.

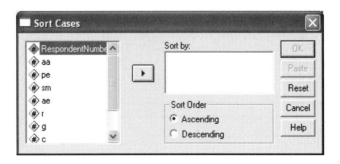

Figure 5.10   Sort Cases Dialog Box

Click on the variable in the list on the left that you want to use as the key (in this case, the variable "RespondentNumber"), and then click on the button with the right arrow. Then click the **OK** button, and finally save the data file. Do this for both files, using the same key each time. Sorting the data and then merging them using a unique key ensures that the data from the two files are merged so that the data for the first respondent that resides in the first file is matched with the data for the first respondent that resides in the second file. The data are also similarly matched for the second respondent, the third respondent, and so on. After all, analyses would produce incorrect results if the data from the first respondent that is in the first file were matched with data from the second file that belonged to some other respondent.

Once the two data files have been prepared, open the first file. Then, from the **Data** pull-down menu select **Merge Files**, and then select **Add Variables** . . . You will see a dialog box that asks you to enter the name of the second file to be merged. Enter the name of this file and click the **Open** button. The dialog box shown in Figure 5.11 will appear.

Next, select **Match cases on key variables in sorted files**, click on the key variable (in our example, this would be the variable "RespondentNumber") in the box on the left, and then click on the button with the right-hand arrow that is just to the left of the **Key Variables** box. Click the **OK** button to merge the two files. As before, you may want to save this new combined file (perhaps giving it a new

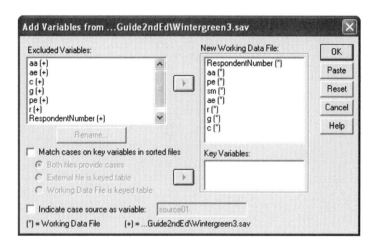

Figure 5.11 Add Variables Dialog Box

file name) to have a single data file with all the records (and thus be able to skip the step of merging the two files the next time you want to conduct an analysis using all of the cases). Again, it is also a good idea to list a few cases using the **Case Summaries . . .** command to see that you have correctly instructed SPSS how to merge the data.

EXERCISE FOUR

Iversen and Norpoth (1987) presented hypothetical data gathered in an effort to answer the question, "Does the mass media raise the public's concern with the economy by their coverage of economic news?" The data were gathered in an experiment in which subjects were randomly assigned to an experimental and a control group. Each group watched a television newscast made up of actual stories shown on the evening news. The experimental group watched a newscast that included a story on the state of the economy, and the control group watched a newscast that did not include this story. Members of each group then filled out a questionnaire that included a 10-point rating scale used to measure the importance subjects placed on the "state of the economy."

(Continued)

Suppose that the data have been entered into two different files by two different people and that the first person entered the data for the experimental group and the second person entered the data for the control group. To conduct the data analyses, the two datasets need to be integrated into one.

Using the data below, create and save a dataset for each of the two groups. Then append them into one dataset. List the data to confirm that the data were merged correctly.

Control group subject		Experimental group subject	
Number	Rating	Number	Rating
01	5	06	7
02	4	07	5
03	4	08	6
04	4	09	6
05	3	10	6

EXERCISE FIVE

In Exercise Three, we computed an average based on three test scores. Suppose that a fourth test is given and stored in a separate dataset. Using the following data, create this new dataset, and then merge the two datasets into one that contains all four test scores for each student. List the data to confirm that the data were merged correctly.

Student	
Number	Test 4
01	80
02	75
03	95
04	80
05	85

CHAPTER 6

Using SPSS to Perform Statistical Analyses

Chapter Purpose

This chapter illustrates several examples of using SPSS to perform statistical analyses.

Chapter Goal

To provide readers with skills to perform fundamental statistical analyses using SPSS.

The power of SPSS lies in its ability to perform complex statistical analyses of large datasets, saving the researcher countless hours of computation. This chapter illustrates the easy-to-use pull-down menu approach to instruct SPSS to perform the analyses typically covered in a first-level statistics course. Each technique will be introduced by a research question, followed by a discussion of how to use SPSS to conduct the analysis. Output from the analysis will be presented and interpreted, and an answer to the research question will be given.

FREQUENCY DISTRIBUTIONS

Refer to Chapter 3 for a discussion of frequency distributions (the Frequencies dialog box was illustrated in Figure 3.11, and the results from a frequency distribution were presented in Figure 3.12). As a brief reminder, the frequency distribution was obtained as follows: From the

Analyze pull-down menu, select Descriptive Statistics, and then select Frequencies . . .

CORRELATION

We are interested in the question, "In the Wintergreen study, to what extent are academic ability and parent education related to one another?" If they are related, then a change in one variable would tend to be accompanied by a change in the other variable. One way to assess whether or not there is a relationship between these two variables is to look at a scatterplot of the data. The following chart is patterned after Lewis-Beck (1995, p. 19), and it shows each individual case when it is graphed using Parent Education for the X-axis and Academic Ability for the Y-axis. To obtain this scatterplot using SPSS, from the Graphs pull-down menu, select Scatter . . . You will see the Scatterplot dialog box asking you to choose a type of scatterplot. Click on Simple and then the Define button. Choose variable "aa" for the Y-axis and choose variable "pe" for the X-axis. Next, click the Titles . . . button, type "Scatterplot" for Title Line 1, type "Academic Ability and Parent Education" for Title Line 2, and click the Continue button. Click the OK button, and take a look at the chart that is produced (see Figure 6.1).

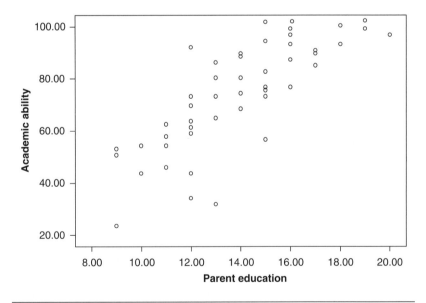

Figure 6.1   Scatterplot of Academic Ability and Parent Education

As you can see from this scatterplot, there appears to be a relationship between academic ability and parent education, so that increased levels of one variable are associated with increased levels of the other. However, it would be nice to have a statistical measure of the strength of this relationship. The *correlation coefficient* is a statistic commonly used to assess the strength of a relationship between two variables that are linearly related to one another (you can see the linear pattern in the scatterplot, as opposed to a pattern with a curved, exponential, or some other shape). The correlation coefficient always ranges from −1 to +1 (regardless of the units of measurement of the variables). A coefficient of 0 indicates that there is no relationship between the variables (this will be illustrated by a random pattern in the scatterplot); a coefficient of +1 indicates a perfect direct relationship (an increase in one variable is associated with an increase in the other); and a coefficient of −1 indicates a perfect inverse relationship (an increase in one variable is associated with a decrease in the other).

To obtain the correlation coefficient, from the **Analyze** pull-down menu, select **Correlate,** and then choose **Bivariate . . .** You will see the Bivariate Correlations dialog box shown in Figure 6.2.

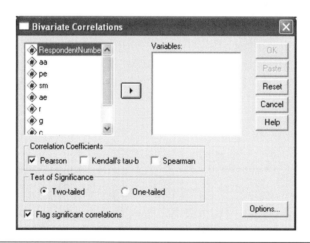

Figure 6.2   Correlations Dialog Box

Select the variables "aa" and "pe," choose the **Pearson** correlation coefficient, choose the **two-tailed** test of significance, and choose **Flag significant correlations**. Click **OK** to run the Correlation procedure. You will obtain the output shown in Figure 6.3.

Correlations

		aa Academic ability	pe Parent education
aa Academic ability	Pearson correlation	1	.793**
	Sig. (2-tailed)	.	.000
	N	50	50
pe Parent education	Pearson correlation	.793**	1
	Sig. (2-tailed)	.000	.
	N	50	50

**Correlation is significant at the 0.01 level (2-tailed).

Figure 6.3   Results From Correlation Procedure

From this output, we can see that academic ability and parent education have a correlation of .793, which indicates a rather strong relationship between the two variables. Indeed, SPSS tells us that with 50 cases, a correlation of this size is statistically significant at the $p < .0005$ level (which is printed as .000 in the middle portion of the output). Note that in the comment at the bottom of the output, SPSS reports that the correlation is significant at the 0.01 level, although we know from the reported p-value that the result is significant at even more stringent criteria.

CROSSTABULATION AND CHI-SQUARE

One of the most common ways of looking at the association between two categorical variables (that is, variables whose values represent different categories, such as the "Gender" variable) is to use the *chi-square* statistic. We are interested in the question, "In the Wintergreen study, are students from urban communities rated similarly to those from rural communities in terms of their advisor evaluation?" To answer this question, we would *crosstabulate* the two variables and look at the percentage of students from each community type who were evaluated in each of the three categories of likelihood to succeed. We would then test the similarity of the two distributions using the chi-square statistic.

To create the crosstabulation using SPSS, from the **Analyze** pull-down menu, select **Descriptive Statistics,** and then choose **Crosstabs . . .** You will see the Crosstabs dialog box shown in Figure 6.4.

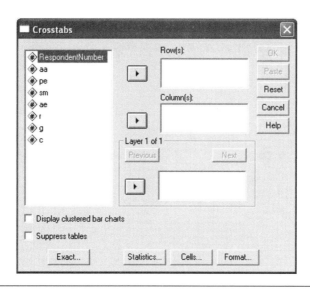

Figure 6.4   Crosstabs Dialog Box

Select Community Type ("c") for the row variable and Advisor Evaluation ("ae") for the column variable. Click the **Statistics . . .** button. In the **Crosstabs: Statistics** dialog box, click the box next to **Chi-Square**, and then click the **Continue** button. Next, click the **Cells . . .** button. Click on the **Observed Count** box, as you will be interested in the number of cases in each cell of the table. Next, click the **Row Percentages** box. You could choose the other percentages as well, but this is the one that is of interest, since you want to know the percentage of students from urban (and rural) communities in each category of advisory evaluation, not the other way around. Click the **Continue** button, and then click the **OK** button. The tables shown in Figure 6.5 will appear in the Viewer window.

Case Processing Summary

	Cases					
	Valid		Missing		Total	
	N	Percent	N	Percent	N	Percent
c Community type* ae Advisor evaluation	50	100.0%	0	.0%	50	100.0%

c Community type* ae Advisor evaluation Crosstabulation

			ae Advisor evaluation			
			.00 Fail	1.00 Succeed or fail	2.00 Succeed	Total
c Community type	.00 Urban	Count	9	14	7	30
		% within c Community type	30.0%	46.7%	23.3%	100.0%
	1.00 Rural	Count	4	11	5	20
		% within c Community type	20.0%	55.0%	25.0%	100.0%
Total		Count	13	25	12	50
		% within c Community type	26.0%	50.0%	24.0%	100.0%

Chi-Square Tests

	Value	df	Asymp. Sig. (2-sided)
Pearson Chi-Square	.642[a]	2	.725
Likelihood Ratio	.656	2	.720
Linear-by-Linear Association	.320	1	.571
N of Vaild Cases	50		

a. 1 cells (16.7%) have expected count less than 5. The minimum expected count is 4.80.

Figure 6.5   Results From Crosstabs Procedure

Let's look at this output for a moment. On the far-right-hand side of the table, we see that 30 students are from urban communities and 20 students are from rural communities. Along the bottom of the table, we see that 26% of the students were rated as likely to fail, 50% of the students were rated as could either succeed or fail, and 24% of the students were rated as likely to succeed. This *marginal count* and *marginal percentage* (that is, the count and percentage in the margins of the table) contain the same information that we saw in the results from the frequency distributions obtained earlier.

Now let's look at the row for the students from urban communities. Among these 30 students, 30% were rated as likely to fail, 47% of the students were rated as could either succeed or fail, and 23% of the students were rated as likely to succeed. Among the 20 students from rural communities, 20% were rated as likely to fail, 55% of the students were rated as could either succeed or fail, and 25% of the students were rated as likely to succeed. These percentages look somewhat different, but are they different enough that they are unlikely to have been distributed this way due to chance alone? To answer that question, SPSS provides a number of different chi-square statistics. For this example, we will use the familiar Pearson chi-square, which for this table has a value of .642 with two degrees of freedom. The probability associated with this chi-square value is .725, far exceeding the .05 level of significance. Thus, we conclude that students from urban and rural communities were rated similarly in their advisor evaluations.

TESTING HYPOTHESES ABOUT TWO MEANS (*t*-TEST)

Frequently, we are interested in whether or not two groups have the same mean on some variable. We are interested in the question, "Did males and females in the Wintergreen study have similar mean academic ability scores?" To test the hypothesis of equality of means for two groups, we can use the *t-test* statistic.

To have SPSS compute this statistic, from the **Analyze** pull-down menu, select **Compare Means**, and then choose **Independent-Samples *t*-Test . . .** The following dialog box shown in Figure 6.6 will appear.

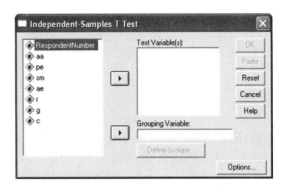

Figure 6.6   Independent Samples *t*-Test Dialog Box

Select Academic Ability ("aa") as the **Test Variable** (that is, the *dependent variable*), and select Gender ("g") as the grouping variable (that is, the *independent variable*). Then click the **Define Groups . . .** button to tell SPSS which values represent each of the two groups. Because our grouping variable was coded as either "0" or "1," enter "0" for "Group 1" and "1" for "Group 2." Click the **Continue** button to return to the previous dialog box, and then click the **OK** button to run the procedure. The results shown in Figure 6.7 will appear in the Viewer window.

Group Statistics

	g Gender	N	Mean	Std. Deviation	Std. Error Mean
aa Academic ability	.00 Male	28	70.7500	17.55758	3.31807
	1.00 Female	22	72.1818	17.61395	3.75531

Independent Samples Test

		Levene's Test for Equality of Variances		t-test for Equality of Means						
									95% Confidence Interval of the Difference	
		F	Sig.	t	df	Sig. (2-tailed)	Mean Difference	Std. Error Difference	Lower	Upper
aa Academic ability	Equal variances assumed	.345	.560	−.286	48	.776	−1.43182	5.00921	−11.50351	8.63988
	Equal variances not assumed			−.286	45.174	.776	−1.43182	5.01118	−11.52378	8.66014

Figure 6.7   Results From Independent Samples *t*-Test Procedure

Notice that SPSS first reports the means, standard deviations, and standard error of the means for each of the two groups (males had a mean of 70.8, and females had a mean of 72.2). Because there are two different ways to compute the *t*-test (depending on whether or not the two groups have similar variances on the dependent variable), SPSS computes Levene's Test for Equality of Variances to determine which method should be used. In our example, this test yields a probability of .56, and since this probability is greater than .05, we conclude that the variances are not statistically significantly different from one another and that *t*-test statistic should be based on equal variances. Next, we see the *t*-tests for differences in the two means. Because we just decided to use the equal-variance method, we read the results from the first line of the *t*-tests (labeled "Equal variances assumed"). The result is a *t*-value of −.29, with 48 degrees of freedom, and a probability of .78. As this is greater than .05, we conclude that males and females had similar mean academic ability scores.

Let's take one more look at these results. You can see from the results that the difference between the means of the two groups is −1.43. While this is the observed difference, the true difference is likely to be either a little more or a little less than this amount. Thus, in the right-hand columns of the table, SPSS has provided the upper and lower bounds on the 95% confidence interval for this difference. As you can see, we can be 95% sure that the true difference in the means is somewhere between −11.5 and 8.6.

The type of *t*-test we just performed is known as a *t-test for independent samples*, as we were comparing means for two different groups. However, what if we were comparing means for two different variables that were measured for each case? For example, suppose that for each student in the Wintergreen study, we had measured both mother's and father's level of education, and now we want to compare the means of these two variables. In this situation, we would conduct a *t-test for related sample*, as the two variables are related to each other in that both were measured for each student. To have SPSS perform this analysis, from the **Analyze** pull-down menu, select **Compare Means**, and then choose **Paired-Samples *t*-Test . . .** SPSS will then ask you to choose the variables to be paired for the analysis. You can run the analysis once you have selected the variables by clicking the **OK** button.

COMPARING SEVERAL MEANS (ANOVA): ONE GROUP

The *t*-test is used to compare variable means for members of two different groups. However, if we are interested in an independent variable that has more than two groups, then we will need to use the analysis of variance (ANOVA) procedure. We would conduct an ANOVA to answer the question, "Do students in each of the three groups of religious affiliation have similar mean academic ability scores?" Because we have only one independent variable, we have SPSS conduct what is known as a *one-way ANOVA.* From the **Analyze** pull-down menu, select **Compare Means**, and then choose **One-Way ANOVA . . .** You will see the dialog box shown in Figure 6.8.

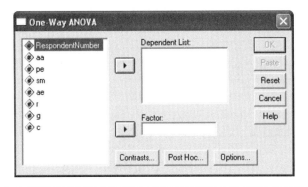

Figure 6.8   *One-Way ANOVA Dialog Box*

Select Academic Ability ("aa") as the dependent variable and Religious Affiliation ("r") as the factor (that is, the independent variable). The results of the ANOVA procedure will tell us whether or not there is a difference among at least two of the groups, but it will not tell us which of the groups exhibited this difference. Therefore, click the **Post Hoc . . .** button to select a post hoc method for determining which groups (if any) are different. Let's choose **Scheffe** as a conservative post hoc comparison. Click the **Continue** button to return to the previous dialog box, and then click the **Options . . .** button. In the **Statistics** box, choose **Descriptive** to get descriptive statistics and **Homogeneity of Variance** in order to test whether or not the three groups had equal variances (an assumption of the ANOVA procedure). Now click the **Continue** button to return to the original dialog box, and then click the **OK** button to run the procedure. You will see these results shown in Figure 6.9 in the Viewer window.

Oneway

Descriptives

aa Academic ability

	N	Mean	Std. deviation	Std. error	95% confidence interval for Mean		Minimum	Maximum
					Lower bound	Upper bound		
.00 Catholic	21	67.4762	15.82599	3.45351	60.2723	74.6801	36.00	93.00
1.00 Protestant	20	76.4000	19.24468	4.30324	67.3932	85.4068	29.00	99.00
2.00 Jewish	9	69.3333	15.63650	5.21217	57.3141	81.3526	48.00	96.00
Total	50	71.3800	17.41673	2.46310	66.4302	76.3298	29.00	99.00

Test of Homogeneity of Variances

aa Academic ability

Levene statistic	df1	df2	Sig.
.267	2	47	.767

ANOVA

aa Academic ability

	Sum of squares	df	Mean square	F	Sig.
Between groups	861.742	2	430.871	1.446	.246
Within groups	14002.038	47	297.916		
Total	14863.780	49			

Figure 6.9 (Continued)

Post Hoc Tests

Multiple Comparisons

Dependent Variable: aa Academic ability Scheffe

(I) r Religious affiliation	(J) r Religious affiliation	Mean difference (I-J)	Std. error	Sig.	95% confidence Interval	
					Lower bound	Upper bound
.00 Catholic	1.00 Protestant	−8.92381	5.39280	.264	−22.5561	4.7085
	2.00 Jewish	−1.85714	6.87664	.964	−19.2404	15.5261
1.00 Protestant	.00 Catholic	8.92381	5.39280	.264	−4.7085	22.5561
	2.00 Jewish	7.06667	6.92802	.598	−10.4465	24.5798
2.00 Jewish	.00 Catholic	1.85714	6.87664	.964	−15.5261	19.2404
	1.00 Protestant	−7.06667	6.92802	.598	−24.5798	10.4465

Homogeneous Subsets

aa Academic ability

Scheffe[a,b]

r Religious affiliation	N	Subset for alpha = .05
		1
.00 Catholic	21	67.4762
2.00 Jewish	9	69.3333
1.00 Protestant	20	76.4000
Sig.		.390

Means for groups in homogeneous subsets are displayed.

a. Uses Harmonic Mean Sample Size = 14.373

b. The group sizes are unequal. The harmonic mean of the group sizes is used. Type I error levels are not guaranteed.

Figure 6.9   Results From One-Way ANOVA Procedure

The first table in Figure 6.9 displays the results for the descriptive statistics showing the number and mean academic ability score for the students within each religious affiliation as well as for the total group of students. Other descriptive statistics that are presented include the standard deviation, the standard error of the mean, the upper and lower bounds of the 95% confidence interval for the mean, and the minimum and maximum academic ability scores.

The second table displays the results of Levene's test of homogeneity of variance. The test statistic is .27 with 2 and 47 degrees of freedom and a probability of .77. Since this probability is greater than the commonly used cut of .05, we conclude that the three groups have equal variances (and thus, that this assumption for the analysis of variance has not been violated).

The third table displays the results of the overall analysis of variance, including the between-groups, within-groups, and total sum of squares, degrees of freedom, and mean squares. The F-ratio for this analysis is 1.446, with a probability of .246. As this exceeds our requirement of a probability less than .05 for statistical significance, we conclude that students in the three groups of religious affiliation had similar mean academic ability scores. (This can also be seen in the overlapping ranges defined by the 95% confidence intervals for the means.)

The fourth table displays the results of the post hoc comparisons. Had the overall ANOVA been significant, we would have needed to look for which pairs of means were different using the post hoc comparison. As you can see, SPSS repeats that there were no significant differences (for example, the mean difference between Catholics and Protestants is 8.9, with a standard error of 5.4 and a probability of .26). In the fifth table, all three means are presented in a single table of homogenous subsets of means, as the groups do not differ from each other in their means.

COMPARING SEVERAL MEANS (ANOVA): TWO OR MORE GROUPS

Now let's look at an example of an analysis of variance where there are two independent variables. Suppose we were interested in examining the effect of both gender and religious affiliation on academic ability, as well as the interaction between these two variables. In other words, "Do males and females have different academic abilities, do students with different religious affiliations have different academic abilities, and do the results for males and females depend on whether we are looking at students of one or another religious affiliation?" To conduct this *two-way* analysis of variance (so known as there are two independent variables in the analysis), from the **Analyze** pull-down menu, select **General Linear Model**, and then choose **Univariate . . .** You will see the following dialog shown in Figure 6.10.

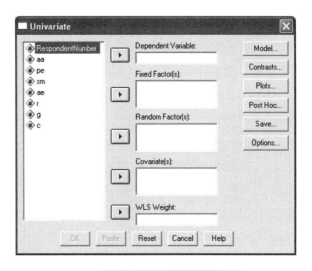

Figure 6.10   Univariate ANOVA Dialog Box

Select Academic Ability ("aa") as the **Dependent Variable** and Gender and Religious Affiliation ("g" and "r") as the **Fixed Factor(s)** (that is, the independent variables in a fixed effects model). Click the **OK** button to run the analysis, and the results shown in Figure 6.11 will appear in the Viewer window.

First, look at the results for the *r*g interaction* between the two variables. We see that the F-ratio associated with the interaction effect is 1.36, with a probability of .27. Thus, we conclude that there is no interaction between the two variables, so that the effect of one

Univariate Analysis of Variance

Between-Subjects Factors

		Value label	N
r Religious affiliation	.00	Catholic	21
	1.00	Protestant	20
	2.00	Jewish	9
g Gender	.00	Male	28
	1.00	Female	22

Tests of Between-Subjects Effects

Dependent Variable: aa Academic ability

Source	Type III sum of squares	df	Mean square	F	Sig.
Corrected model	1691.125[a]	5	338.225	1.130	.359
Intercept	213580.508	1	213580.508	713.413	.000
r	622.497	2	311.248	1.040	.362
g	40.309	1	40.309	.135	.715
r * g	813.393	2	406.697	1.358	.268
Error	13172.655	44	299.379		
Total	269619.000	50			
Corrected total	14863.780	49			

a. R-Squared = .114 (Adjusted R-Squared = .013)

Figure 6.11   Results From Univariate ANOVA Procedure

variable does not depend on the level of the other (that is, whether or not there is a difference between males and females does not depend on their religious affiliation). Because there is no interaction, we next look at the *main effects*. For the Gender variable, the F-ratio is .14, with a probability of .72. Thus, we conclude that there was no difference between males and females. For the variable of Religious Affiliation, the F-ratio is 1.0, with a probability of .36. Thus, we conclude that there was no difference among Catholic, Protestant, and Jewish students.

You will note that this ANOVA procedure did not provide the means for the variables. To obtain the means (which we would want to present in the results of the ANOVA), from the **Analyze** pull-down menu, we can select **Compare Means** and then choose **Means . . .** The dialog box shown in Figure 6.12 will appear.

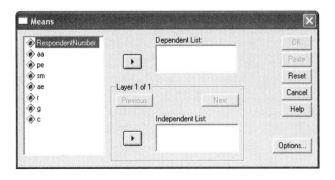

Figure 6.12   Means Dialog Box

Select Academic Ability ("aa") for the **Dependent List** and Gender ("g") and Religious Affiliation ("r") for the **Independent List**. Click the **OK** button to run the procedure. The results shown in Figure 6.13 will appear in the Viewer window.

If we want the means of one variable based on levels of the other (which we would if we had a significant interaction effect), then in the **Means** dialog box, we would select Religious Affiliation for the **Independent List**, click the **Next** button to get to the second **Layer**, select Gender for the next variable, and click the **OK** button to run the procedure.

Means

Case Processing Summary

	Cases					
	Included		Excluded		Total	
	N	Percent	N	Percent	N	Percent
aa Academic ability * r Religious affiliation	50	100.0%	0	.0%	50	100.0%

Report

aa Academic ability

r Religious affiliation	Mean	N	Std. deviation
.00 Catholic	67.4762	21	15.82599
1.00 Protestant	76.4000	20	19.24468
2.00 Jewish	69.3333	9	15.63650
Total	71.3800	50	17.41673

Figure 6.13   Results From Means Procedure

The results from this procedure will detail the means for males and females within each level of religious affiliation (that is, the means for Catholic males and females, Protestant males and females, and Jewish males and females). Means, numbers of cases, and standard deviations will be presented. Totals within each group, as well as totals across all groups, will also be presented.

SIMPLE REGRESSION

Earlier, we examined the correlation between academic ability and level of parent education. You may recall that there was a rather strong, and statistically significant, correlation. We will now conduct a *simple regression* analysis to answer the question, "How well can we predict academic ability if we know something about parent education?"

To conduct this analysis, from the **Analyze** pull-down menu, select **Regression**, and then choose **Linear . . .** The dialog box shown in Figure 6.14 will appear.

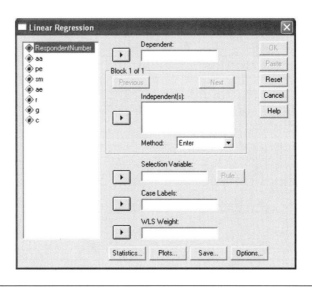

Figure 6.14   Regression Dialog Box

Select Academic Ability ("aa") as the dependent variable and Parent Education ("pe") as the independent variable. You will also note that SPSS provides for many important options that are useful in conducting regression analysis, which are available via the **Statistics . . . , Plots . . . , Save . . .** , and **Options . . .** buttons. Readers interested in learning more about regression analysis are encouraged to review Schroeder, Sjoquist, and Stephan (1986), as well as the chapters on regression in the SPSS manuals (which detail these analysis options). Click the **OK** button to run the procedure. The results shown in Figure 6.15 will appear in the Viewer window.

Regression

Variables Entered / Removed[b]

Model	Variables entered	Variables removed	Method
1	pe Parent education[a]		Enter

a. All requested variables entered
b. Dependent Variable: aa Academic ability

Model Summary

Model	R	R square	Adjusted R square	Std. error of the estimate
1	.793[a]	.629	.621	10.71733

a. Predictors: (Constant), pe Parent education

ANOVA[b]

Model		Sum of squares	df	Mean square	F	Sig.
1	Regression	9350.443	1	9350.443	81.406	.000[a]
	Residual	5513.337	48	114.861		
	Total	14863.780	49			

a. Predictors: (Constant), pe Parent education
b. Dependent Variable: aa Academic ability

Coefficients[a]

Model		Unstandardized coefficients		Standardized coefficients	t	Sig.
		B	Std. Error	Beta		
1	(Constant)	1.659	7.875		.211	.834
	pe Parent education	5.045	.559	.793	9.023	.000

a. Dependent Variable: aa Academic ability

Figure 6.15   Results From Regression Procedure

This output presents quite a bit of useful information (Lewis-Beck, 1995, pp. 41–53, presented the results of the regression analysis, which are summarized below). First, let's recall that the purpose of the regression analysis is to create an equation that will allow us to predict values of a *criterion* (or dependent variable) from values of a *predictor* (or independent variable). In our example, we are interested in being able to predict a student's level of academic ability (the criterion) based on knowledge about parents' level of education (the predictor). Thus, our prediction equation takes the theoretical form of

$$Y = a + bX + e$$

where "Y" is the value of the criterion, "a" is the intercept of the regression line (the value of "Y" when "X" is zero), "b" is the slope of the line (also known as the *regression coefficient*), "X" is the value of the predictor, and "e" is the error term (since we are unlikely to have a perfect prediction). From the "Coefficients" table in the output shown above, we see that the value of the intercept is 1.66 and the value of the regression coefficient is 5.05 (the error term is important in the theoretical regression equation, but as we are unable to actually measure it, we cannot assign it a value in the computed regression equation). Thus, our prediction equation is

$$Y' = 1.66 + 5.04X$$

where Y' is the predicted value of academic ability, given a particular level of parent education and our regression equation.

Let's think about what this means. If a student's parents have no education, then we would expect the student to get 1.66 items correct on the 100-item academic ability test. However, in this case, the intercept does not particularly contribute to the analysis (other than to serve a mathematical function) in that no student in the dataset has a parent education level of less than 9 years. The regression coefficient gives us an idea of the importance of parent education level. Specifically, as the slope of the line tells how much change we can expect in the criterion variable given a unit change in the predictor variable, we understand that for every additional year of parent education, a student can be expected to get 5.04 additional items correct on the test of academic ability.

We are also interested in knowing how well the regression equation performs in predicting the criterion. The most popular summary measure of this is *R-squared* (also known as the *coefficient of determination*). Remember, in regression analysis, we are interested in fitting a single line through the data so that prediction errors will be minimized. The *R*-squared statistic tells us how well the prediction line fits the data. If *R*-squared equals 0, then there is no relationship between the predictor and criterion variables. If there is a perfect relationship between the two variables, then *R*-squared will equal 1. Usually, *R*-squared falls between 0 and 1.

Let's think a little more about the *R*-squared statistic. If we were predicting a student's academic ability score with no other information about that student, then our best guess would simply be the average score for the group of students. However, for any given student, there will be some deviation from this mean score. Thus, each student's score may be thought of as the following:

Difference between an individual score and the mean
   = Difference between the predicted score and the mean
     + Difference between the individual score and the predicted score

If we square the difference (that is, the deviation) between each student's individual score and the mean score, and then add all the resulting squared deviations, then we have what is known as the *total sum of squared deviations* (TSS) about the mean. Since we know something about parent education, we are able to improve our prediction through the use of the regression equation (as opposed to simply predicting a student's score by using the mean). Thus, we can take the difference between each student's predicted score and the mean score, square those differences, and add all the results. This will give us what is known as the *regression sum of squared deviations* (RSS). Finally, the difference between the students' actual scores and their predicted scores from the regression equation represents the error that remains. If we take this difference for each student, square that difference, and then add the results for all students, then we have what is know as the *error sum of squared deviations* (ESS) (also known as *residual sum of squared deviations*).

R-squared is then defined as RSS divided by TSS. From the "Model Summary" table in Figure 6.15, we see that *R*-squared equals .63.

Substantively, 63% of the variation in academic ability can be accounted for by level of parent education, given our linear regression model (if one were quite confident in the theoretical basis for this model, one might say that 63% of the variation in academic ability is *explained* by level of parent education). If you would like to do some of the calculating yourself, SPSS provides the necessary details in the "ANOVA" table. Notice that the regression sum of squares is 9350.4 and the residual (that is, the error) sum of squares is 5513.3. Adding the two, we find that the total sum of squares is 14,863.7. If we divide the regression sum of squares by the total sum of squares (9350.5/14,863.7) we find that *R*-squared is .629.

Because we are interested in extrapolating from our sample data to the population as a whole, we are also interested in testing whether or not the intercept and the regression coefficient are significantly different than zero. Using the logic of the *t*-test, we can test the significance of the intercept and the regression coefficient. As we see in the "Coefficients" table, the *t*-value for parent education is 9.02, with a probability far less than .05. Thus, we conclude that parent education is highly related to academic ability in the student population. However, we note a nonsignificant finding for the test of the intercept, which suggests that it might well be zero in the population as a whole.

As with any other estimate, we may prefer to establish a *confidence interval* around the estimate rather than relying solely on the estimate itself. You can see from the SPSS output that the standard error for the regression coefficient is .56. Thus, we can build a 95% confidence interval using the following equation:

$$5.04 \pm 2.01(.56)$$

where 5.04 is the regression coefficient, 2.01 is the *critical value of t* with 48 degrees of freedom, and .56 is the standard error of the estimate of the regression coefficient. Thus, we can be 95% confident that the regression coefficient in the population lies somewhere between 3.91 and 6.17.

Let's look at one more statistic presented in the output, the *standard error of the estimate* (SEE). This is the standard deviation of the *residuals* (the residuals are the differences between the actual and predicted scores, and thus reflect the error in the prediction equation). The SEE is something like an average prediction error for the model (the SEE would be 0 if there were no prediction error). However, as the SEE does not have an upper bound, it is difficult to use it as a measure of overall model quality. Thus, R-squared may be preferred over SEE, as it can range only from 0 to 1. You may see in the Model Summary that the SEE in this example is 10.7. As Lewis-Beck (1995) noted,

> In the case at hand, SEE = 10.7 exam items, suggesting that on average the model generates a fair amount of prediction error. If the researcher's goal is merely to predict test outcomes, this indicates that the equation will not do strikingly well. (p. 49)

At this point, we have gathered from the SPSS output the information we need to present the results of the regression analysis:

The prediction equation is $Y' = 1.66 + 5.04X$

t-value for the constant = .21, not significant

t-value for the regression coefficient = 9.02, $p < .001$

R-squared = .63

Number of cases = 50

Standard Error of the Estimate = 10.72

USING NONPARAMETRIC STATISTICS

Techniques such as ANOVA and regression are known as *parametric techniques*, and they are based on several assumptions (for example, that the data are measured on at least an interval scale, that the data are normally distributed, etc.). However, the researcher will at times encounter data that do not meet these assumptions, and at those times the many available *nonparametric* methods will come in handy. These methods typically have few or no assumptions, and therefore one can use them in a variety of situations (such as when the data are nominal or ordinal in nature or when they do not follow a normal distribution). SPSS provides several statistical tests based on nonparametric methods. I have included mention of the ability of SPSS to conduct nonparametric analyses, as it provides the researcher with a wealth of methods to analyze data that are not appropriate for parametric techniques, and I encourage readers to explore this interesting and useful branch of statistics (see for example, Gibbons, 1985, 1993).

As an example, let's compare academic ability scores for males and females, but let's use a test that compares medians instead of using a *t*-test to compare means. From the **Analyze** pull-down menu, select **Nonparametric Tests**, and then choose **K Independent Samples . . .** ("K" means that we are looking at two or more samples). The dialog box shown in Figure 6.16 will appear.

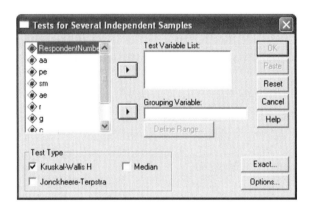

Figure 6.16   Nonparametric Tests Dialog Box

Select Academic Ability ("aa") as the **Test Variable** and Gender ("g") as the **Grouping Variable**. Use the **Define Range . . .** button to define the minimum and maximum values for the grouping variable (because of the way gender was coded in our example, enter "0" and "1"). In the **Test Type** box, choose the **Median** test. Click the **OK** button to run the procedure, and the results shown in Figure 6.17 will appear in the Viewer window.

To conduct the median test, SPSS first computes the overall median (the point that divides the distribution of scores in half) for all 50 students. Next, a two-by-two "Frequencies" table is created in which the number of students above the median and the number at or below the median are displayed for the students in each group. Finally, the chi-square test is applied to the table (the results are printed in the "Test Statistics" table). In our example, the probability associated with this test is greater than .05, and we therefore conclude that males and females have similar median scores on the academic ability test.

Median Test

Frequencies

		g Gender	
		.00 Male	1.00 Female
aa Academic ability	> Median	11	14
	< = Median	17	8

Test Statistics[a]

		aa Academic ability
N		50
Median		72.5000
Chi-Square		2.922
df		1
Asymp. Sig.		.087
Yates' continuity correction	Chi-Square	2.029
	df	1
	Asymp. sig.	.154

a. Grouping Variable: g Gender

Figure 6.17   Results From Nonparametric Tests, Median Test Procedure

EXERCISE SIX

Sirkin (1999, p. 273) presented an example in which a random sample of 10 university students (Group 1) was rated on a tolerance index designed to measure tolerance of "unpopular" beliefs (with a score of "0" meaning lowest level of tolerance and a score of "15" meaning highest level of tolerance). The same index was then used to measure the tolerance of another sample of students from the same university who had recently attended a workshop on multicultural diversity (Group 2). Using the data below, conduct a *t*-test for independent samples to answer the question, "Is there a difference between these two groups of students in their levels of tolerance?"

	Student	
Number	Group	Score
01	1	2
02	1	3
03	1	3
04	1	4
05	1	4
06	1	5
07	1	5
08	1	5
09	1	6
10	1	6
11	2	4
12	2	4
13	2	4
14	2	5
15	2	5
16	2	6
17	2	6
18	2	7
19	2	7
20	2	7

·EXERCISE SEVEN

Sirkin (1999) continued with the example of a random sample of university students who are military veterans. These veterans were given a workshop designed to influence participant tolerance levels by subjecting them to criticism of their own attitudes. The before-and-after tolerance scores are presented below. Conduct a *t*-test for dependent samples to answer the question, "Are tolerance scores for this group different at the end of the workshop than they were at the beginning?"

	Student	
Number	Before	After
01	4	3
02	4	4
03	4	6
04	5	7
05	5	6
06	6	4
07	6	8
08	7	9
09	7	7
10	7	8

EXERCISE EIGHT

Sirkin (1999, p. 281) provided an example in which employees at an advertising firm were being trained to properly advise and assist clients. The firm was interested in whether employees in the training were more or less satisfied depending on the time of the training. Thirty employees were randomly assigned to one of three different classes: a class that met one hour a day from Monday through Friday, a class that met at night under similar circumstances, and a class that met for a single session on Saturday (for

(Continued)

5 hours of training plus time for breaks and meals). At the end of instruction, each person rated his or her overall satisfaction on a scale of "0" *(dissatisfied)* to "5" *(completely satisfied)*. Using the data below, conduct a one-way ANOVA and a Scheffe post hoc comparison to answer the question, "Are students in the three different training classes equally satisfied, and if not, where are the differences between the groups?" The data were coded so that "1" represents the day class, "2" represents the night class, and "3" represents the Saturday class.

	Employee	
Number	Format	Satisfaction
01	1	5
02	1	5
03	1	5
04	1	5
05	1	4
06	1	4
07	1	4
08	1	4
09	1	3
10	1	2
11	2	5
12	2	4
13	2	4
14	2	3
15	2	3
16	2	2
17	2	2
18	2	2
19	2	1
20	2	0
21	3	5
22	3	5
23	3	5
24	3	4
25	3	4
26	3	4
27	3	3
28	3	3
29	3	3
30	3	2

EXERCISE NINE

Iversen and Norpoth (1987, p. 38) presented an example in which 12 subjects were randomly assigned to one of four groups. Each subject then watched a newscast about economic issues. Two of the groups watched a newscast about unemployment, and two of the groups watched a newscast about inflation. Of the two groups that watched the story about unemployment, one saw a newscast with positive coverage, and one saw a newscast with negative coverage (there was a similar division of the two groups that saw a newscast about inflation). After watching the newscast, subjects were asked to rate the importance of the economy as an issue on a scale of "1" to "10." Using the data below, conduct a two-factor ANOVA to answer the question, "Does subject rating of the importance of the economy as an issue depend on whether subject watched a newscast with coverage of unemployment or inflation, on whether subject watched a newscast with positive or negative coverage, or on an interaction between these two variables?" The data were coded so that the type of story is coded "1" if it was about unemployment and "2" if it was about inflation, and the tone of the story is coded "1" if it was positive and "2" if it was negative.

Subject number	Type of story	Tone of story	Score
01	1	1	1
02	1	1	2
03	1	1	3
04	2	1	5
05	2	1	6
06	2	1	7
07	2	2	7
08	1	2	8
09	1	2	9
10	1	2	7
11	2	2	7
12	2	2	10

EXERCISE TEN

Lewis-Beck (1980) provided hypothetical data that could have been gathered from local government employees in the town of Riverside (a hypothetical medium-sized Midwestern city). Thirty-two of the 306 employees were randomly selected and interviewed. Data were obtained regarding current annual income and number of years of formal education. Conduct a regression analysis using these data to answer the question, "Do employees with more formal training receive better pay?"

Respondent	Education	Income
01	04	06281
02	04	10516
03	06	06898
04	06	08212
05	06	11744
06	08	08618
07	08	10011
08	08	12405
09	08	14664
10	10	07472
11	10	11598
12	10	15336
13	11	10186
14	12	09771
15	12	12444
16	12	14213
17	12	16908
18	12	18347
19	13	19546
20	14	12660
21	14	16326
22	15	12772
23	15	17218
24	16	12599
25	16	14852
26	16	19138
27	16	21779
28	17	16428
29	17	20018
30	18	16526
31	18	19414
32	20	18822

CHAPTER 7

Using the SPSS Syntax Window

Chapter Purpose

This chapter introduces the use of SPSS syntax.

Chapter Goal

To provide readers with an understanding of SPSS syntax, an opportunity to learn basic coding skills, and an understanding of the value of learning SPSS syntax.

Chapter Glossary

Debugging: The process of correcting mistakes in program code.

Program Structure: The logical organization of an SPSS program; good logical organization helps ensure programming ease and efficiency.

SPSS Program: A set of lines of SPSS code that can be run from the Syntax Editor to read, manipulate, and analyze data.

Syntax Editor: SPSS window in which command syntax can be written and edited.

USING THE SYNTAX WINDOW

So far, we have worked with SPSS using pull-down menus. While this is a very convenient way to work with the software, if at some later time you wish to repeat an analysis that was done using pull-down menus, you will have to redo each step in the analysis. You can avoid this duplication of effort by creating and saving a syntax file of SPSS commands. In addition, there are procedures and options that are available to you through the use of SPSS syntax that are not available through the pull-down menus.

There are two ways to use the syntax window. The first is to open the **Syntax Editor** window and type SPSS commands directly into it. This is a good way to write SPSS programs, but it does require that you be familiar with the syntax of SPSS commands. The second method is to use the **Paste** button that appears in analysis procedure dialog boxes.

Let's try an example of the second method. Once again, click on the **Analyze** pull-down menu, select **Descriptive Statistics**, and select **Frequencies . . .** You will see the dialog box illustrated in Figure 3.11 (of course, if you have chosen different variables, or exited and reentered SPSS since we looked at this example, then you will need to reopen the dataset and select these variables). Now click the **Paste** button. SPSS will open a syntax window and insert into it the following lines of code:

```
FREQUENCIES
  VARIABLES = sm ae r g c
  /ORDER = ANALYSIS.
```

Let's study these three lines of SPSS syntax. The word **FREQUEN-CIES** is an *SPSS command* that instructs SPSS to create a frequency distribution (notice that it begins at the far-left column of the window). The expression **VARIABLES =** is an *SPSS subcommand* that instructs SPSS to analyze the variables that are listed on that line (notice that it is indented at least one space). The expression **ORDER =** is an SPSS subcommand that instructs SPSS to organize the output by analysis (so that a single statistics table is displayed for all variables, rather than a separate table for each variable). The SPSS command ends when it encounters a period. The **FREQUENCIES** command has many more subcommands available. You can learn more about them from the SPSS manual or by using the **Help** pull-down menu.

Go ahead and save this file. From the **File** pull-down menu, select **Save.** Since this is the first time the syntax has been saved, you will see the **Save As** dialog box. Enter a file name (such as "Wintergreen1.sps," since this is the syntax file for the first analysis of the Wintergreen data) in the dialog box. Now, highlight these three lines in the syntax window (using the standard Windows procedure of holding down the "Shift" key and using the cursor movement keys or by using the mouse). You can now tell SPSS to run these commands by clicking the "Run Current" toolbar icon (see Figure 7.1). This is the "right arrow" icon— it is the fourth one from the right on the toolbar.

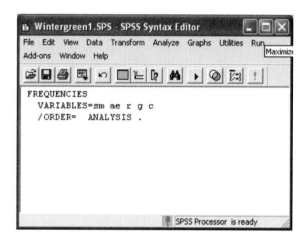

Figure 7.1   SPSS Syntax Editor With Code for Frequencies Procedure

As an alternative, instead of clicking the toolbar icon, you can run the highlighted commands by holding down the "Ctrl" key on the keyboard and simultaneously press the "R" key (i.e., enter the "Ctrl-R" keystroke combination). As a third option, you can run the commands from the **Run** pull-down menu.

Once the syntax has run, you will see the results in the Viewer window. Now, if you finish your SPSS session for today but decide tomorrow that you want to run the same analysis, all you have to do is open the dataset, open this syntax file, and highlight and run the code in the syntax window. This will save you from having to repeat the several keystrokes involved in using the dialog boxes. While this may not seem like a terrific savings with only three lines of code, it becomes increasingly important as your SPSS programs become longer and more complicated.

We have now covered two different ways of running SPSS: using the pull-down menus and using the syntax window. Neither one is right or wrong, and neither one is better than the other. Rather, it is important to be able to use both approaches, as sometimes one method is easier than another. For quick, simple analyses it may be easier to work with the pull-down menus. For more involved analyses that may be run several times (with or without variations each time), it is far less time-consuming to use the syntax window. You may discover that you would like to switch back and forth between the two methods. This can be easily accomplished, as the pull-down menus are available to you even in the syntax window (they also remain available to you in the Data Editor window). For example, you may wish to both paste SPSS code into a syntax file using the pull-down menus and to insert comments into the file by typing them in directly.

It is worth studying the code that SPSS pastes into the syntax window, as this will give you many insights into how SPSS works. In particular, compare what is written in the syntax and what appears in the output. This will help you build your programming and data analysis skills.

THE STRUCTURE OF BASIC SPSS PROGRAMS

You will find it easiest to write SPSS syntax if you approach this task with a certain structure with a logical flow. Some elements of this structure will be included in most every program you write, while other elements will appear in only some of your programs. Following this structure will also make it easy to review your program at some later date and remember why you wrote that program and what the program does. While you can create whatever structure works best for you, I recommend that you start with the following:

- ○ Commenting about the program as a whole
- ○ Reading the data
- ○ Manipulating the data
- ○ Labeling variables
- ○ Labeling values of variables
- ○ Analyzing the data

DEBUGGING SPSS PROGRAMS

SPSS programs are rarely written so well that they run the first time without any problems. It is much more likely that SPSS will encounter errors as your program runs, and these errors will likely cause your program to stop running. Don't worry about it! When SPSS encounters an error, it generates a message to you. Just take a look at the output, and use the error message(s) as a guide to what the problem might be. These messages typically show up right after the error occurs, and they contain clues as to what the error was. Thus, their placement and content provide clues about what was wrong in the program. Chances are, you forgot a slash or a period, left out a quotation mark, or used the wrong syntax in an SPSS command. If you have multiple errors, it is best to look at (and correct) the ones that occur first. It may be that an error at one step in the program caused many subsequent errors and all that is required is the correction of the first error.

Once you have identified the problem, edit the program in the Syntax Editor to make the correction, and then run the program again. Either the program will work this time or it won't. In either case, if you have corrected some of the errors, then you have made progress. If there are more errors, simply repeat the process of looking at the error messages, correcting the mistake in the Syntax Editor, and running the program again.

This process of error correction is called *debugging* the program. Get used to it, as it is part of the programming activity. With practice, it becomes easier and like a game.

INSERTING COMMENTS ABOUT THE PROGRAM

There are differing styles among people who write computer programs. For example, some write programs in so cryptic a manner that no one else can figure them out. In contrast, some people prefer that their programs be easily understood by others who look at them. I encourage you to adopt the latter attitude. For one thing, the person most likely to be looking at the program will be you, and you don't want to have to spend much time figuring out your own work from a couple of weeks (or months, or years) ago. Another reason for making your programs easily understood is that you may need to give them to someone else to take over, especially if they are programs that are run periodically as new data are collected (for example, if you repeat a survey at the end of every semester). Your colleagues and assistants will appreciate your help in making the program easy to understand.

One of the easiest ways to make your programs understandable is to insert *comments* liberally throughout the program. You can add a comment to a program in the Syntax Editor by inserting an asterisk in the first column of a line; anything between the asterisk and the next period is ignored by SPSS. You may even choose to use multiple asterisks to make an obvious feature, such as a box, to draw attention to the comments. A comment looks like this:

```
**********************************************
* This is a comment about a program      *
* Everything from the first asterisk to  *
* The period is ignored by SPSS          *
**********************************************.
```

READING DATA

If you enter and save data using the SPSS Data Editor, then the data are saved as an SPSS system file. SPSS knows how to read the data, what the variable and value labels are, and what values have been declared as missing values. Therefore, you can open the dataset at any later time using the **File** pull-down menu and the **Open . . .** command. Similarly, if you are writing code in a syntax window, you can read an SPSS system file with the **GET** command:

```
GET FILE = filename.
```

where *filename* is the name of the file that contains the data. For example,

```
GET FILE = c:\Wintergreen\Wintergreen.sav.
```

would open a dataset on the "c:" drive, in the "Wintergreen" subdirectory, called "Wintergreen.sav."

However, if you are reading data that have been entered as a text file and have not been saved as an SPSS dataset, then you will need to read the data using the **DATA LIST** command. As an example, the following syntax would read the data from Figure 5.1.

```
DATA LIST
   FILE = 'c:\Wintergreen\Wintergreen.txt' FIXED
     RECORDS = 1 TABLE
   /1 RespondentNumber 1-2 aa 4-5 pe 6-7 sm 9-9 ae 10-10
   r 11-11 g 12-12 c 13-13.
```

Notice that SPSS begins reading the data by using the **DATA LIST** command. The **FILE** subcommand tells SPSS the name of the file in which the data are located. The **FIXED** subcommand tells SPSS that the data are in fixed format, the **RECORDS =** subcommand is used to state the number of records for each case, and the **TABLE** subcommand tells SPSS to display a table listing the variable definitions that were given in this command. The data for the first record are then defined (that is, their name and column locations are specified) after the "/1" characters. If a second record were required, the variables in that record would be defined following a "/2"; if a third record were required, the variables in that record would be defined following a "/3," and so on.

MERGING DATA

If you need to append one dataset to another (that is, add new cases rather than new variables), then you can use the following commands:

```
ADD FILES
   /FILE = filename
   /FILE = filename.
```

The **ADD FILES** command instructs SPSS that two files will be appended. The next two lines inform SPSS which two files are to be merged. If you had already opened a dataset using either the pull-down menus or the **GET** command, then you could use an asterisk instead of a file name in one of these lines.

If you need to merge two data files and add variables to existing records, then the following commands may be used. Remember, both files have to be sorted in ascending order by a common key in order to ensure that the records match properly:

```
MATCH FILES
  /FILE = filename
  /FILE = filename
  /BY varlist.
```

The **MATCH FILES** command instructs SPSS that two files will be merged so that variables from one file will be added to another. The next two lines inform SPSS which two files are to be merged (if you had already opened a dataset using either the pull-down menus or the **GET** command, then you could use an asterisk instead of a file name in one of these lines). The final line of the code tells SPSS which variables are to be used to match the cases (for example, a variable whose values were unique case identifiers, such as an identification number).

MANIPULATING THE DATA

Once the data have been read, you may need to manipulate them before conducting your analyses. For example, you may need to recode a variable, do a computation, or select cases to be analyzed. The SPSS code for each of these tasks will be described below.

In Chapter 4, we recoded the academic ability variable into a new variable that contained grouped values of the original variable (see Figure 4.1). The following code would accomplish the same task if it were written and run in a syntax window:

```
RECODE
  aa
  (0 thru 1 = 0)    (10 thru 19 = 1)   (20 thru 29 = 2)
  (30 thru 39 = 3)   (40 thru 49 = 4)   (50 thru 59 = 5)
  (60 thru 69 = 6)   (70 thru 79 = 7)   (80 thru 89 = 8)
  (90 thru 99 = 100) INTO   aa_new.
```

The **RECODE** command is used to start this procedure. This command is followed by the variable that is being recoded, the groupings of the old values and their associated new values, and the name of the new variable that will have the recoded values. As an interesting exercise, repeat the steps in Chapter 4 using the **Transform, Recode, Into Different Variables . . .** pull-down menus, ending with the **Paste** button, to write the recode syntax into the Syntax Editor. Then repeat the steps in Chapter 4 using the **Transform, Visual Bander . . .** pull-down menus, ending with the **Paste** button to write the visual banding syntax into the Syntax Editor. Now compare the two sets of code and notice their similarities and differences.

In Chapter 4, we also computed a variable for parent education ("par_ed") by taking the average of mother's education ("mom_ed") and father's education ("dad_ed"). If you pasted the content of the dialog box in Figure 4.8, the following code would appear in the syntax window:

```
COMPUTE par_ed = (mom_ed + dad_ed)/2
```

The **COMPUTE** command is used to start this procedure. This command is followed by the variable that is being computed, and then the variables and operations that are to be used for the computation.

Finally, in Chapter 4 we looked at how to select cases to be included in an analysis without deleting those cases that were not selected. This was called *filtering* the data. When SPSS filters data, it includes in analyses those cases for which the specified filter variable has values of "1," and it does not include those cases that have a value of "0." Since we are filtering the data by selecting students from rural communities and we are using a variable for community type (named "c") that is coded as "0" for "urban" and "1" for "rural," we can filter the data by simply using the following command:

```
FILTER BY c.
```

However, if you repeat the steps that you took in Chapter 4 (see Figure 4.9) and then click the **Paste** button, the following code will be written to the syntax window:

```
USE ALL.
COMPUTE filter_$ = (c = 1).
VARIABLE LABEL filter_$ 'c = 1 (FILTER).'
VALUE LABELS filter_$ 0 'Not Selected' 1 'Selected.'
FORMAT filter_$ (f1.0).
FILTER BY filter_$.
EXECUTE.
```

Let's take a close look at this code. SPSS begins by using all the data in the dataset rather than some subset of the data. SPSS then creates a new variable called "filter_$" and assigns this variable the value of "1" if our condition is satisfied (that is, if the student comes from a rural community) and a value of "0" if our condition is not satisfied. SPSS then labels the new variable and its values and formats the variable as having a numeric format one digit wide with no decimal points. SPSS then "filters" the dataset, so that only those cases that meet our condition are used in the analysis. Finally, SPSS executes these lines of code (SPSS does not automatically execute the code for data manipulations, but does when you run a procedure such as Frequencies). If you wish, later on you can tell SPSS to use all the cases in an analysis, or you can select cases based on some other criteria.

You may recall that in the **Select Cases** dialog box, there was the option for those cases that were not selected to be "deleted" rather than "filtered." In this case, SPSS uses a different command:

```
SELECT IF(c = 1).
```

Those cases that were not selected are dropped from the active dataset. The advantage to this approach is that it reduces the size of the dataset and consequently speeds up the analyses. The disadvantage is that you cannot reselect the deleted cases. Also, if you unintentionally resave the dataset without giving it a new name, you will have to do your data entry over again.

SAMPLE SPSS PROGRAM

In Chapter 3, we had SPSS create descriptive summaries and frequency distributions for the Wintergreen data (see Figures 3.9 and 3.11). Let's do that once again, but this time let's write a complete program using the syntax window (assume that the data have been stored in a text file called "Wintergreen.txt" that is located in the "Wintergreen" directory on the "c:" drive). You can write this program by pasting from the pull-down menus and dialog boxes, or you can write it by typing directly into the syntax window. The program will look like this (if you run this program, you will again see the results shown in Figures 3.10 and 3.12).

```
*
* This program analyzes data for the Wintergreen College study of
* variables that contribute to student academic success on a first-year
* entrance exam
*       List cases
*       Descriptive statistics
*       Frequency distributions
* This study is based on hypothetical data from Lewis-Beck, 1995
*.
*
* Read the data
*.
DATA LIST FILE = 'c:\Wintergreen\Wintergreen.txt' FIXED RECORDS = 1 TABLE
   /1 resp_num 1-2 aa 4-5 pe 6-7 sm 9-9 ae 10-10 r 11-11 g 12-12
      c 13-13.
*
* Assign variable and value labels
*.
variable labels
  resp_num 'Respondent number'/
  aa         'Academic ability'/
  pe         'Parent education'/
  sm         'Student motivation'/
  ae         'Advisor evaluation'/
  r          'Religious affiliation'/
  g          'Gender'/
  c          'Community type'.
value labels
  sm 0 'Not willing'
     1 'Undecided'
     2 'Willing'/
  ae 0 'Fail'
     1 'Succeed or fail'
     2 'Succeed'/
  r   0 'Catholic'
      1 'Protestant'
      2 'Jewish'/
  g   0 'Male'
      1 'Female'/
  c   0 'Urban'
      1 'Rural'.
*
* Conduct the analyses
*       List cases, frequency distributions, descriptive statistics
```

```
*.
list variables = resp_num aa pe sm ae r g c
   /cases = from 1 to 5 by 1.
descriptives variables = aa pe
   /statistics = mean stddev min max.
frequencies variables = sm ae r g c.
```

Let's look at this program. The first thing to notice is it follows the structure and style described earlier in this chapter. First, there is a comment about the program as a whole, so that the next time you look at it, you will remember something about it (in this example, I have stated the purpose of the program, the procedures that will be run, and the source of the data). Next, the data are read, and variable and value labels are assigned. Had it been necessary, I could have assigned missing values or made any transformations after the data were read. Finally, the analyses of interest are performed: cases are listed, descriptive statistics are computed, and frequency distributions are created. In those situations where it makes sense, you can conduct some of the analyses, then perform the data transformations, and then conduct further analyses.

Now let's look at two elements of the style of this program. First, note that all the code is written in a very orderly manner, using common levels of indenting (I suggest you use the space bar, rather than the Tab key, to indent lines of code). For example, in the variable labels section, all the variable names start in the same column, and all the variable labels start in the same column. Similarly, in the value labels section, all the variable names start in the same column, and for each of the variables, all the value labels start in the same column. While this is not a requirement of SPSS coding, it does make the program easy to read and understand. This is an important feature when it comes time to debug the program or to review it at some later date. The second stylistic element to note is the liberal use of comments throughout the program. This may not truly be necessary in a program that is as short and simple as our example, but you will find that it is most helpful as your programs grow in length and complexity.

CORRELATION

In Chapter 6, we had SPSS compute the correlation between the Academic Ability and Parent Education variables (see Figures 6.2 and 6.3).

If you repeat those steps using the pull-down menus and then click the **Paste** button, the following code will appear in the syntax window:

```
CORRELATIONS
  /VARIABLES = aa pe
  /PRINT = TWOTAIL NOSIG
  /MISSING = PAIRWISE.
```

SPSS uses the **CORRELATIONS** command to begin this procedure. Next, the variables to be correlated are specified on the **VARIABLES** subcommand. This is followed by the **PRINT** subcommand, which instructs SPSS to print the two-tailed test of statistical significance in an annotation. Finally, the **MISSING** subcommand tells SPSS to treat missing data using *pairwise deletion,* in which the correlation will be calculated as long as a case has values for the two variables being correlated. This is not as critical in our example with only two variables, but it can be more important if several variables are being correlated with one another. As an alternative, SPSS can handle missing data using *listwise deletion,* in which a case will be deleted from all analyses if it has data missing for any of the variables in the list.

CROSSTABULATION

In Chapter 6, we had SPSS display a crosstabulation of community type by advisor evaluation and compute the chi-square statistic for this crosstabulation (see Figure 6.4). If you repeat those steps using the pull-down menus and then click the **Paste** button, the following code will appear in the syntax window:

```
CROSSTABS
  /TABLES = c  BY ae
  /FORMAT = AVALUE TABLES
  /STATISTIC = CHISQ
  /CELLS = COUNT ROW
  /COUNT ROUND CELL.
```

SPSS uses the **CROSSTABS** command to begin this procedure. The **TABLES** subcommand tells SPSS what variables to use to create the table (the row variable is listed first, and the column variable is listed second). The **FORMAT** subcommand instructs SPSS on how to print the table (this command is not an essential part of the syntax, and if you leave it out, SPSS will use default values). The **STATISTIC** subcommand instructs SPSS to compute the chi-square statistics, the **CELLS** subcommand instructs SPSS to display the observed frequency and row percentage in each cell of the table, and the **COUNT** subcommand instructs SPSS to round case weights. If you run this syntax, you will see output that was presented earlier in Figure 6.5.

t-TEST FOR INDEPENDENT SAMPLES

In Chapter 6, we had SPSS compute a *t*-test for independent samples to compare mean academic ability between males and females (see Figure 6.6). If you repeat those steps using the pull-down menus and then click the **Paste** button, the following code will appear in the syntax window:

```
T-TEST
  GROUPS = g(0 1)
  /MISSING = ANALYSIS
  /VARIABLES = aa
  /CRITERIA = CIN(.95).
```

SPSS uses the **T-TEST** command to begin this procedure, followed by the **GROUPS** subcommand, which specifies the independent variable and the coded values of the two groups. Next, the **MISSING** subcommand instructs SPSS how to handle missing data (you can omit this subcommand if you write your own code, allowing SPSS to use its default value). The **VARIABLES** subcommand tells SPSS which variable is to be used for the dependent variable (you may specify more than one dependent variable in order to instruct SPSS to perform a series of *t*-tests). Finally, the **CRITERIA** subcommand tells SPSS what level of significance to use (in this example, SPSS will base the statistical test on a 95% confidence level, which is the same as an alpha level of .05). You can also omit this subcommand when you write your own code, allowing SPSS to use its default value. If you run this syntax, you will see output that was presented in Figure 6.9.

ANOVA

In Chapter 6, we had SPSS compute an analysis of variance (ANOVA) in order to compare mean academic ability among students of differing religious affiliation (see Figure 6.8). If you repeat those steps using the pull-down menus and then click the **Paste** button, the following code will appear in the syntax window:

```
ONEWAY
   aa BY r
   /MISSING ANALYSIS
   /POSTHOC = SCHEFFE ALPHA(.05).
```

SPSS uses the **ONEWAY** command to begin this procedure, followed by the dependent variable and the independent variable. The **MISSING** command instructs SPSS in how to handle missing cases. In this example, SPSS has been instructed to delete cases for which there is missing data for the dependent variable or grouping variable. The **POSTHOC** subcommand instructs SPSS to conduct a Scheffe post hoc test with an alpha of .05. If you run this syntax, you will see output that was presented in Figure 6.9.

In Chapter 6, we also had SPSS compute a factorial ANOVA in order to simultaneously compare mean academic ability among males and females and among students of differing religious affiliation (see Figure 6.10). If you repeat those steps using the pull-down menus and then click the **Paste** button, the following code will appear in the syntax window:

```
UNIANOVA
   aa BY g   r
   /METHOD = SSTYPE(3)
   /INTERCEPT = INCLUDE
   /CRITERIA = ALPHA(.05)
   /DESIGN = g r g*r.
```

SPSS uses the **UNIANOVA** command to begin this procedure, followed by the dependent variable and the independent variables. The **METHOD** subcommand tells SPSS how to assess the effects (by using the SSTYPE(3) specification, SPSS uses the Type III sum-of-squares method as the computational method for partitioning the sums of squares). The **CRITERIA** subcommand tells SPSS to use the .05 criteria in building the model, and the **DESIGN** subcommand specifies the effects to be included in the model. If you run this syntax, you will see output that was presented in Figure 6.11. I will leave the computation of means (see Figures 6.12 and 6.13) as an exercise for the reader.

REGRESSION

In Chapter 6, we had SPSS compute a regression analysis in order to predict academic ability from level of parent education (see Figure 6.14). If you repeat those steps using the pull-down menus and then click the **Paste** button, the following code will appear in the syntax window:

```
REGRESSION
  /MISSING LISTWISE
  /STATISTICS COEFF OUTS R ANOVA
  /CRITERIA = PIN(.05) POUT(.10)
  /NOORIGIN
  /DEPENDENT aa
  /METHOD = ENTER pe.
```

SPSS uses the **REGRESSION** command to begin this procedure. Next, the **MISSING** subcommand instructs SPSS how to handle missing cases (in this example, SPSS is instructed to delete a case if it is missing data for any of the variables to be included in the analysis). The **STATISTICS** subcommand tells SPSS which statistics to compute. The **CRITERIA** subcommand tells SPSS what level of statistical significance to use in building the regression model. The **NOORIGIN** subcommand tells SPSS not to suppress the constant in the regression equation (in contrast, **ORIGIN** requests that the regression line be constructed through the origin). The **DEPENDENT** subcommand identifies the dependent variable. The **METHOD** subcommand instructs SPSS how to construct the regression model. If you run this syntax, you will see output that was presented in Figure 6.15.

NONPARAMETRIC STATISTICS

In Chapter 6, we had SPSS compute a nonparametric median test in order to compare the median academic ability between males and females (see Figure 6.16). If you repeat those steps using the pull-down menus and then click the **Paste** button, the following code will appear in the syntax window:

```
NPAR TESTS
  /MEDIAN = aa   BY g(0 1)
  /MISSING ANALYSIS.
```

The **NPAR TESTS** command instructs SPSS to begin this procedure. The first subcommand tells SPSS which nonparametric procedure to use and defines the dependent variable and independent variables (along with the minimum and maximum value for the independent variable). The **MISSING** subcommand tells SPSS to delete cases on a test-by-test basis (when several tests are specified). As an alternative, listwise deletion of cases could be specified. If you run this syntax, you will see output that was presented in Figure 6.17.

CHAPTER 8

Next Steps

Chapter Purpose

This chapter introduces additional features of SPSS and sources of additional information.

Chapter Goal

To provide readers with opportunities to further advance their SPSS skills.

By now you have become familiar with the fundamental operations of SPSS. In this chapter, I offer direction for the next steps you may take in your study of this statistical software package. First, we will look at the various ways you can receive help in SPSS. Next, I will introduce the SPSS manuals. I encourage you to explore them and become proficient at using them as reference tools. The SPSS "Statistics Coach" will then be introduced, followed by mention of Pivot Tables, SPSS utilities, the SPSS Production Facility, the SPSS Script Facility, and the SPSS World Wide Web home page.

HELP IS NEARBY

There are a number of ways you can get help in SPSS. You will find your understanding of SPSS and your skills as an SPSS user will improve if you take advantage of these sources of help.

You can run the SPSS help facility by going to the **Help** pull-down menu and selecting **Topics.** You may browse the contents of the Help window by clicking on the **Contents** tab, or search using the **Index** or **Search** tabs (see Figure 8.1).

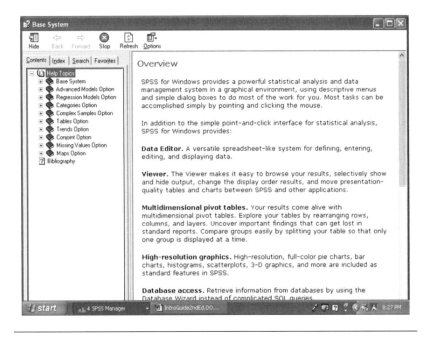

Figure 8.1   Base System Help Window

You can run the SPSS tutorial by going to the **Help** pull-down menu and selecting **Tutorial.** Use the arrows in the bottom-right-hand corner of the window to follow the tutorial lessons (see Figure 8.2).

You can run the SPSS tutorial by going to the **Help** pull-down menu and selecting **Case Studies.** Use the arrows in the bottom-right-hand corner of the window to follow the examples provided (see Figure 8.3).

You can click the **Help** button within a dialog box to instruct SPSS to provide information about that dialog box. Doing so takes you directly to that topic in the Help window.

You can obtain **Pivot table context help** by activating (double-clicking) a pivot table in the Viewer and then right-clicking on the

Figure 8.2   SPSS Tutorial

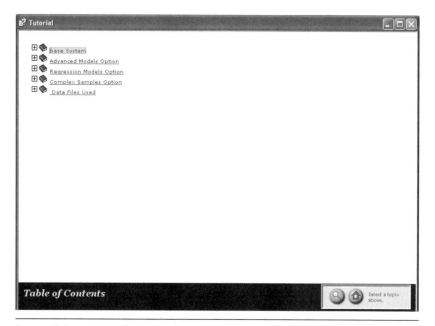

Figure 8.3   SPSS Case Studies

pivot table. Select **What's this?** from the context menu, and you will see definitions of the terms in the table. Similarly, you can click on any part of a dialog box with the right mouse button to get context-specific help (see Figure 8.4).

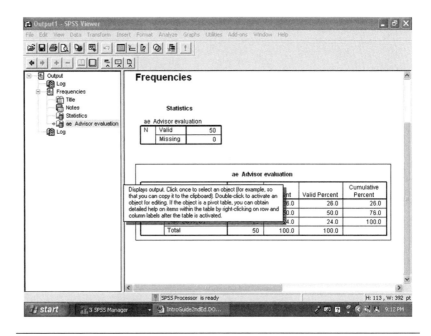

Figure 8.4 Pivot Table Context Help

You can look up information in the **SPSS manuals** included on your SPSS CD. In addition, the SPSS Syntax Reference Guide is already installed on your computer. From the **Help** pull-down menu, select **Command Syntax Reference**. There is a great wealth of information in the manual that will help you become a strong SPSS user, and I encourage you to use it often (see Figure 8.5).

Feel free to use any of these methods of getting help anytime you feel the need for more information.

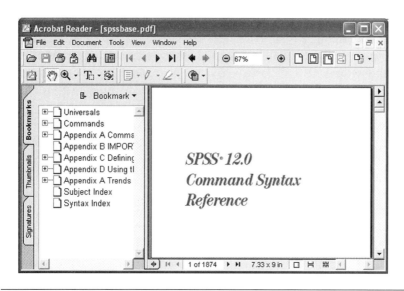

Figure 8.5   SPSS Command Syntax Reference

GETTING THE MOST FROM THE SPSS MANUALS

Although they may appear somewhat daunting, you will get the most from the SPSS manuals if you think of them as your friends. Keep them by your side, and they will remain ever ready to help out when you find yourself in need of an answer. The manuals are particularly useful when you are uncertain about the function of a procedure available to you through the pull-down menus or when you are uncertain about what is being requested in a dialog box. By referring to the manuals, you will gain a greater mastery over the SPSS software, and you will improve your ability to make sure that your output provides you with the results you need. In addition, as you find yourself using the syntax window with increasing frequency, you will be pasting code from dialog boxes that looks cryptic to you. By referring to the manuals, you will learn what this code means (or more precisely, what output you will get as a result of using this code). It is worth repeating that the more familiarity you have with the meaning of SPSS code, the greater the mastery you will have of the software. As an added benefit of studying the manuals, the SPSS code, and the contents of your output, you will also increase your understanding of statistical procedures. I strongly encourage you to develop your facility at running SPSS from the syntax window and to use the manuals to help you increase your programming skills.

Another important reason for using the SPSS manuals is that the software is capable of many functions that are available to you only through the syntax window (that is, they are not available through the pull-down menus and dialog boxes). If you are limited in your understanding of SPSS by what you know about the pull-down menus, you will not have complete control over the many procedures SPSS has to offer. Again, think of the manuals as your friends, waiting to expand your horizons.

One other reason for studying the manuals is that they will help you to understand the options you have for controlling how the SPSS software runs. There are many *options* you can set that control how SPSS runs during the time you are using it (that is, during an SPSS *session*), and you may find that you like some options more than others. You will find it helpful to spend some time with the manuals discovering what the options are and how they function. Of course, you will also need to spend time running SPSS using these different options in order to learn which ones you like the best. You may choose among various options by going to the **Edit** pull-down menu and selecting **Options . . .** The dialog box shown in Figure 8.6 will appear.

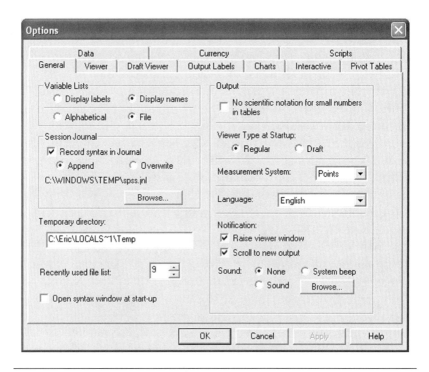

Figure 8.6   SPSS Options Dialog Box

SPSS software comes as a "base system" and several "modules." The base system is the core of SPSS, and every user has access to it. You have access only to the modules that you have purchased in addition to the base system. This modular approach allows users to purchase only the collection of SPSS procedures that they need. Each module comes with its own manual, and I will mention three of them below:

○ The *SPSS Base 12.0 User's Guide* (SPSS, Inc., 2003a) provides an overview of the SPSS software and covers in detail many of the operations available via the pull-down menus.

○ The *SPSS 12.0 Command Syntax Reference* (SPSS, Inc., 2003b) provides specific details of each of the SPSS commands that are available in the base system. Think of this book as a lexicon that will help you understand the SPSS language. You are not likely to read this book from cover to cover. However, I hope that you refer to it often, as it is where you will learn about the many commands that are available to you via the syntax window. As I mentioned above, this manual is available to you via the **Help** pull-down menu.

○ The *SPSS Advanced Modules 12.0* (SPSS, Inc., 2003c) covers the operations of frequently encountered advanced statistics, such as the general linear model that we have used to conduct a simple factorial analysis of variance (ANOVA).

Of course, you will also want to become familiar with the manuals that come with any of the other modules to which you have access. Also, as the manuals are comprehensive and may appear rather lengthy and imposing, you may find them somewhat more manageable if you review their content before diving right into them.

Now, let's take a look at some examples of how to use the manuals.

User's Guide

Suppose you are planning to conduct a regression analysis, but you are uncertain about all the options available to you or you need to better understand what SPSS is requesting in one or another dialog box. Turn to Chapter 26 ("Linear Regression") in the *SPSS Base 12.0 User's Guide.* There, you will find a brief review of the regression procedure. You will also find sample output and details about how to obtain a linear regression analysis, including data considerations, sample output, variable selection methods, defining rules for selection in the analysis, regression plots, options for saving new variables, regression statistics, and other regression options.

Consider the many nonparametric analyses that SPSS is capable of computing. If you are new to this branch of statistics, or if it has been a while since you worked with these techniques, you will find Chapter 34 ("Nonparametric Tests") in the *SPSS Base 12.0 User's Guide* helpful as you identify which techniques are available in SPSS and make decisions about how to appropriately use these methods.

Syntax Reference Guide

One very important function of the *SPSS 12.0 Command Syntax Reference* is to help you understand SPSS syntax. As you paste SPSS code from the dialog boxes into the syntax window, you will encounter commands that are foreign to you. What do you do in this case? Simply refer to this manual. As an example, suppose you paste the SPSS code from the *t*-test procedure and you encounter the subcommand "**/CRITERIA = CI(0.95)**," but you are not sure what this means. In the manual, turn to the **T-TEST** section and look for this subcommand. All sections in this manual begin with a list of the available subcommands, so you will first find the **CRITERIA** subcommand mentioned at the beginning of the section. Later, you will find the subcommand defined as follows:

CRITERIA resets the value of the confidence interval. Keyword CI is required. You can specify a value between 0 and 1 in the parentheses. The default is 0.95. (From *SPSS 12.0 Command Syntax Reference*, p. 1584. Copyright 2003 by SPSS, Inc.)

At this point, you know not only what this subcommand means but also that you can reset the critical value for statistical significance if you so desire.

Another very important function of the *SPSS 12.0 Command Syntax Reference* is to make you aware of those commands that are available to you only when you use the syntax window. Looping functions are one example ("**DO IF**" and "**LOOP—END LOOP**"). I will leave it up to you to discover other examples for yourself.

As I mentioned earlier, you will get the most from the SPSS manuals if you think of them as your friends. Refer to them often for answers to questions and to learn more about how SPSS runs and what it can do for you. Happy reading!

NEXT STEPS

The purpose of this book has been to introduce you to the SPSS software package. Now that you have become familiar with SPSS, I encourage you to learn more about what it has to offer. In this section, I mention some topics you may find of interest. Readers wishing to explore intermediate and advanced skills may find them introduced in *Next Steps With SPSS* (Einspruch, 2004).

Statistics Coach

SPSS provides an interactive "coach" to help users select the appropriate statistical method for analyzing their data. From the **Help** pulldown menu, select **Statistics Coach** to launch the Statistics Coach (see Figure 8.7).

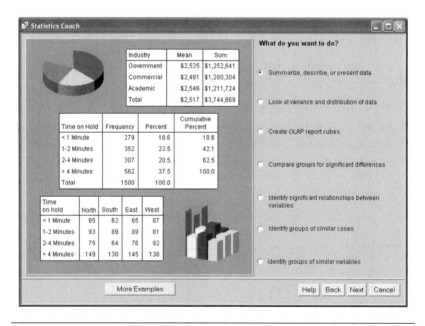

Figure 8.7   SPSS Statistics Coach

The coach prompts the user for information about the kind of analysis to perform, the kind of data to be included in the analysis, and the type of results to be produced. Based on the user's responses to these prompts, SPSS makes a suggestion for the analysis to perform and opens the dialog box for that analysis. This coach is a useful guide for statistical analysis, and it can help users develop their understanding of statistical methodology and its application. Readers seeking help selecting statistical tests are also referred to Kanji (1993).

Pivot Tables

Many SPSS procedures produce results that appear in the Viewer window in the form of pivot tables (for example, the results produced by the crosstabs procedure). These results display information in rows, columns, and layers, which can be exchanged (that is, a row can be made a column, and a column can be made a row). You can double-click on a table to run the Pivot Table Editor, which can be used to modify pivot tables. Pivot tables can be embedded as ActiveX objects in applications that support this feature. See Chapter 9 in the *SPSS Base 12.0 User's Guide* for a discussion of working with output, and see Chapter 11 for additional information on pivot tables, including how to apply a TableLook.

Utilities

SPSS provides you with a number of utilities, which can be accessed from the **Utilities** pull-down menu. For example, if you select **Variables . . .** from this menu, you will see the Variables dialog box shown in Figure 8.8.

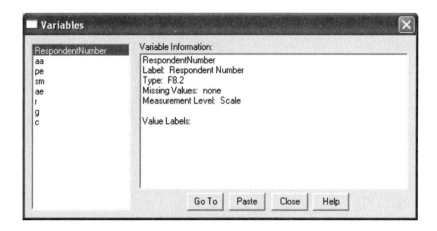

Figure 8.8   Utilities, Variables Dialog Box

This dialog box displays information about each of the variables in the dataset. You may access this information for any given variable by clicking on the variable name on the left-hand side of the dialog box and finding the information on the right-hand side. You may also obtain a list of the variables in the dataset, and information about them, from the **File, Display Data File Information, Working File (External File . . .)** pull-down menu.

You may also add comments to your data file by selecting **Utilities, Data File Comments . . .** to obtain the Data File Comments dialog box. Enter comments that will help you recall important information about the data file, including its source and when it was created. Later, you may review these comments simply by opening the Data File Comments dialog box shown in Figure 8.9.

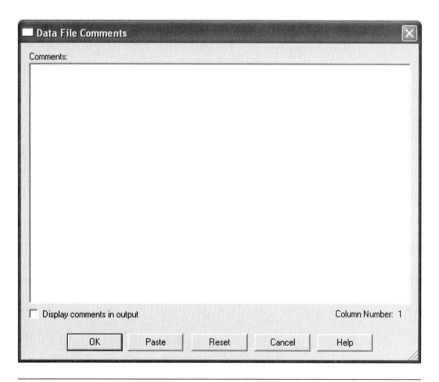

Figure 8.9   Data File Comments Dialog Box

You will find mastery of these utilities helpful as you work with SPSS. More information about SPSS utilities can be found in Chapter 42 of the *SPSS Base 12.0 User's Guide.*

Production and Scripting Facilities

The SPSS Production Facility is described in Chapter 45 of the *SPSS Base 12.0 User's Guide.* This facility allows you to create SPSS syntax files and then run them unattended. This is particularly useful if you routinely run time-consuming analyses. There are many options available in the production facility (which you run from the Windows **Start** menu) that control how production jobs are run and the format of the output they produce.

You can automate SPSS tasks by using the scripting facility. For example, you can automatically customize the output displayed in the Viewer window. See Chapter 46 in the *SPSS Base 12.0 User's Guide* for more information about this facility. Scripts are created or modified in the **Script Window** accessed from the **File** pull-down menu, and scripts are run from the **Utilities** pull-down menu.

World Wide Web Home Page

The World Wide Web address for the SPSS home page is http://www.spss.com. The home page offers news and other information about SPSS. You will find the home page to be a source of interesting information and a place to which you can return to keep up-to-date on developments at SPSS. There is a link to the home page from the **Help** pull-down menu. Of course, you can also access the home page directly from your favorite World Wide Web browser.

CHAPTER 9

Conclusion

This book introduced you to the Statistical Package for the Social Sciences (SPSS), and by now you are able to use SPSS to conduct a variety of statistical analyses. Using the SPSS package takes away the time-consuming tedium of computing statistics by hand and allows the researcher to concentrate on the conceptual aspects of his or her study. Of course, it is still important that the researcher understand the nature and use of statistical techniques, as well as their computational methods. It will always be up to the researcher to choose the appropriate analytic method and to ensure that data collection and data entry have been performed with the highest degree of care. No computer can be responsible for these aspects of a research project.

This book has covered the fundamentals of running SPSS, entering and reading data, transforming data, applying labels, and conducting analyses. It has also introduced you to the SPSS manuals so that you may find information about the additional capabilities of the software package. In addition, I have suggested some next steps for developing your SPSS skills.

Of course, you will want to report the results of your analyses once they have been obtained. In doing so, it is a good idea to keep your audience in mind. If you are writing a report for an academic or technical audience, you will want to follow a traditional style that includes an introduction and statement of the problem, followed by sections on the method, results, discussion, and conclusions of the study. On the other hand, such a style will be cumbersome if you are writing for a nontechnical audience. Instead, you may consider preparing a report that contains an executive summary, an introduction, a section on key findings (remember the value of charts to illustrate findings), and a conclusion. You can complete the report with whatever appendices are necessary to provide interested readers with the technical details or results of the study. If you are preparing the report under contract for a client, you may also get valuable input by having the client review a draft of the report in advance of preparing the final version.

I wish you all the best in your research endeavors, and I hope you come to enjoy SPSS, the broad field of statistics, and the practice of research and evaluation.

Appendix A

Solutions to Exercises

EXERCISE ONE

Codebook for the Data

```
Variable name:     Number
Variable label:    Survey number
Definition:        Unique identifier for each survey

Variable name:     Item_04
Variable label:    Liked book used in class
Values and
value labels:      1  Agree
                   2  Undecided
                   3  Disagree
```

Recoded Data as It Is Entered

```
    Number          Item_04
    01              1
    02              1
    03              2
    04              1
    05              1
    06              2
    07              1
    08              1
    09              1
    10              1
```

Frequencies

Statistics

Liked book used in class

N	Valid	10
	Missing	0

Liked book used in class

		Frequency	Percent	Valid percent	Cumulative percent
Valid	Agree	8	80.0	80.0	80.0
	Undecided	2	20.0	20.0	100.0
	Total	10	100.0	100.0	

Answer to the Research Question

Nearly all (80%) of the students "agreed" that they liked the book that was used in class. The remaining two students were "undecided" whether or not they liked the book. These findings contribute to the teacher's confidence in using the book again in a future class.

EXERCISE TWO

Summarize

Case Processing Summary[a]

	Cases					
	Included		Excluded		Total	
	N	Percent	N	Percent	N	Percent
Subject number	10	100.0%	0	.0%	10	100.0%
Subject age	10	100.0%	0	.0%	10	100.0%
Age group	10	100.0%	0	.0%	10	100.0%

a. Limited to first 100 cases

Case Summaries[a]

		Subject number	Subject age	Age group
1		1.00	17.00	1.00
2		2.00	21.00	2.00
3		3.00	18.00	1.00
4		4.00	23.00	2.00
5		5.00	16.00	1.00
6		6.00	22.00	2.00
7		7.00	17.00	1.00
8		8.00	18.00	1.00
9		9.00	21.00	2.00
10		70.00	19.00	2.00
Total	N	10	10	10

a. Limited to first 100 cases

EXERCISE THREE

Summarize

Case Processing Summary[a]

| | Cases | | | | | |
| | Included | | Excluded | | Total | |
	N	Percent	N	Percent	N	Percent
Student number	5	100.0%	0	.0%	5	100.0%
First test	5	100.0%	0	.0%	5	100.0%
Second test	5	100.0%	0	.0%	5	100.0%
Third test	5	100.0%	0	.0%	5	100.0%
Average of three test scores	5	100.0%	0	.0%	5	100.0%

a. Limited to first 100 cases

		Student number	First test	Second test	Third test	Average of three test scores
1		1.00	90.00	85.00	95.00	90.00
2		2.00	85.00	85.00	85.00	85.00
3		3.00	90.00	80.00	70.00	80.00
4		4.00	70.00	80.00	75.00	75.00
5		5.00	75.00	85.00	80.00	80.00
Total	N	5	5	5	5	5

a. Limited to first 100 cases

EXERCISE FOUR

Summarize

Case Processing Summary[a]

	Cases					
	Included		Excluded		Total	
	N	Percent	N	Percent	N	Percent
Subject number	10	100.0%	0	.0%	10	100.0%
Rating of importance of the economy	10	100.0%	0	.0%	10	100.0%

a. Limited to first 100 cases

Case Summaries[a]

		Subject number	Rating of importance of the economy
1		1.00	5.00
2		2.00	4.00
3		3.00	4.00
4		4.00	4.00
5		5.00	3.00
6		6.00	7.00
7		7.00	5.00
8		8.00	6.00
9		9.00	6.00
10		10.00	6.00
Total	N	10	10

a. Limited to first 100 cases

EXERCISE FIVE

Summarize

Case Processing Summary[a]

| | Cases | | | | | |
| | Included | | Excluded | | Total | |
	N	Percent	N	Percent	N	Percent
Student number	5	100.0%	0	.0%	5	100.0%
First test	5	100.0%	0	.0%	5	100.0%
Second test	5	100.0%	0	.0%	5	100.0%
Third test	5	100.0%	0	.0%	5	100.0%
Average of three test scores	5	100.0%	0	.0%	5	100.0%
Fourth test	5	100.0%	0	.0%	5	100.0%

a. Limited to first 100 cases

Case Summaries[a]

		Student number	First test	Second test	Third test	Average of three test scores	Fourth test
1		1.00	90.00	85.00	95.00	90.00	80.00
2		2.00	85.00	85.00	85.00	85.00	75.00
3		3.00	90.00	80.00	70.00	80.00	95.00
4		4.00	70.00	80.00	75.00	75.00	80.00
5		5.00	75.00	85.00	80.00	80.00	85.00
Total	N	5	5	5	5	5	5

a. Limited to first 100 cases

EXERCISE SIX

Group Statistics

	Group	N	Mean	Std. deviation	Std. error mean
Score on tolerance index	Control	10	4.3000	1.33749	.42295
	Experimental	10	5.5000	1.26930	.40139

Independent Samples Test

		Levene's test for equality of variances		t-test for equality of means						
									95% confidence interval of the difference	
		F	Sig.	t	df	Sig. (2-tailed)	Mean difference	Std. error difference	Lower	Upper
Score on tolerance index	Equal variances assumed	.000	1.000	−.2.058	18	.054	−1.20000	.58310	−2.42504	.02504
	Equal variances not assumed			−.2.058	17.951	.054	−1.20000	.58310	−2.42528	.02528

Answer to the Research Question

The experimental and control groups did not have different mean tolerance scores.

EXERCISE SEVEN

t-Test

Paired Samples Statistics

		Mean	N	Std. deviation	Std. error mean
Pair 1	Tolerance score before workshop	5.5000	10	1.26930	.40139
	Tolerance score after workshop	6.2000	10	1.98886	.62893

Paired Samples Correlations

		N	Correlation	Sig.
Pair 1	Tolerance score before workshop and Tolerance score after workshop	10	.704	.023

Paired Samples Test

		Paired Differences							
					95% confidence interval of the difference				
		Mean	Std. deviation	Std. error mean	Lower	Upper	t	df	Sig. (2-tailed)
Pair 1	Tolerance score before workshop and Tolerance score after workshop	−.70000	1.41814	.44845	−1.71447	.31447	−1.561	9	.153

Answer to the Research Question

The mean tolerance score did not change from before to after the workshop.

EXERCISE EIGHT

Oneway

ANOVA

Satisfaction rating

	Sum of squares	df	Mean square	F	Sig.
Between groups	12.600	2	6.300	4.373	.023
Within groups	38.900	27	1.441		
Total	51.500	29			

Post Hoc Tests

Multiple Comparisons

Dependent Variable: Satisfaction rating Scheffe

(I) Training group	(J) Training group	Mean difference (I-J)	Std. error	Sig.	95% confidence interval	
					Lower bound	Upper bound
Day class	Night class	1.50000*	.53679	.032	.1097	2.8903
	Saturday class	.30000	.53679	.856	−1.0903	1.6903
Night class	Day class	−1.50000*	.53679	.032	−2.8903	−.1097
	Saturday class	−1.20000	.53679	.101	−2.5903	.1903
Saturday class	Day class	−.30000	.53679	.856	−1.6903	1.0903
	Night class	1.20000	.53679	.101	−.1903	2.5903

*The mean difference is significant at the .05 level.

Homogeneous Subsets

Satisfaction rating

Scheffe[a]

Training group	N	Subset for alpha = .05	
		1	2
Night class	10	2.6000	
Saturday class	10	3.8000	3.8000
Day class	10		4.1000
Sig.		.101	.856

Means for groups in homogeneous subsets are displayed.

a. Uses Harmonic Mean Sample Size = 10.000

Answer to the Research Question

There was a difference in the level of satisfaction between partici-pants in the day class and the night class. These were the only two groups that were different from one another.

EXERCISE NINE

Univariate Analysis of Variance

Between-Subjects Factors

		Value Label	N
Type of story	1.00	Unemployment	6
	2.00	Inflation	6
Tone of story	1.00	Positive	6
	2.00	Negative	6

Tests of Between-Subjects Effects

Dependent Variable: Rating of importance of economy as an issue

Source	Type III sum of squares	df	Mean square	F	Sig.
Corrected model	72.000[a]	3	24.000	16.000	.001
Intercept	432.000	1	432.000	288.000	.000
Type	12.000	1	12.000	8.000	.022
Tone	48.000	1	48.000	32.000	.000
Type* tone	12.000	1	12.000	8.000	.022
Error	12.000	8	1.500		
Total	516.000	12			
Corrected total	84.000	11			

a. R-Squared = .857 (Adjusted R-Squared = .804)

ANSWER APPENDIX

Means

Rating of importance of economy as an issue *Type of story

Rating of importance of economy as an issue

Type of story	Mean	N	Std. deviation
Unemployment	5.0000	6	3.40588
Inflation	7.0000	6	1.67332
Total	6.0000	12	2.76340

Rating of importance of economy as an issue *Tone of story

Rating of importance of economy as an issue

Tone of story	Mean	N	Std. deviation
Positive	4.0000	6	2.36643
Negative	8.0000	6	1.26491
Total	6.0000	12	2.76340

Means

Report

Rating of importance of economy as an issue

Type of story	Tone of story	Mean	N	Std. deviation
Unemployment	Positive	2.0000	3	1.00000
	Negative	8.0000	3	1.00000
	Total	5.0000	6	3.40588
Inflation	Positive	6.0000	3	1.00000
	Negative	8.0000	3	1.73205
	Total	7.0000	6	1.67332
Total	Positive	4.0000	6	2.36643
	Negative	8.0000	6	1.26491
	Total	6.0000	12	2.76340

Answer to the Research Question

There was a significant difference between the groups in this study. Participants who saw a story with a negative tone did not rate the importance of the economy as an issue differently depending on the type of story. On the other hand, participants who saw a positive story were more likely to give a higher rating to the importance of the economy as an issue if they saw a story on inflation than if they saw a story on unemployment.

EXERCISE TEN

Regression

Variables Entered/Removed[b]

Model	Variables entered	Variables removed	Method
1	Education (in years)[a]		Enter

a. All requested variables entered

b. Dependent Variable: Income (in dollars)

Model Summary

Model	R	R square	Adjusted R square	Std. error of the estimate
1	.751[a]	.564	.550	2854.60124

a. Predictors: (Constant), Education (in years)

ANOVA[b]

Model		Sum of squares	df	Mean square	F	Sig.
1	Regression	3.16E+08	1	316481758.4	38.838	.000[a]
	Residual	2.44E+08	30	8148748.216		
	Total	5.61E+08	31			

a. Predictors: (Constant), Education (in years)

b. Dependent Variable: Income (in dollars)

Coefficients[a]

Model		Unstandardized coefficients		Standardized coefficients	t	Sig.
		B	Std. Error	Beta		
1	(Constant)	5077.512	1497.830		3.390	.002
	Education (in years)	732.400	117.522	.751	6.232	.000

a. Dependent Variable: Income (in dollars)

Answer to the Research Question

Education and income were strongly related in this study (R-squared equals .56), so that higher number of years of education was associated with higher levels of income.

The prediction equation is $Y' = 5077.5 + 732.4X$

t-value for the constant $= 3.39, p = .002$

t-value for the regression coefficient $= 6.23, p < .001$

R-squared $= .56$

Number of cases $= 32$

Standard error of the estimate $= 2854.60$

Appendix B

Tips

APPROACH

○ Have fun.

○ As you read this book, sit at the computer and try out the skills being discussed, and feel free to experiment.

○ Save your work often. Make backup copies.

DATA ENTRY

○ Plan your dataset before you begin data entry.

○ Use a codebook to help you remember the structure and content of your data.

○ Assign out-of-range values as placeholders for missing data.

○ Approach the task of data entry with the utmost alertness and care in order to keep the data as "clean" as possible.

○ Label your variables and values so your output will be easier to read.

ANALYZING DATA

○ List a few cases before you conduct an analysis to be sure that the data have been read and handled correctly.

○ When merging files (adding variables), be sure to use a key variable.

○ Think about how the choices you make in a dialog box (or in a syntax file) affect what you see in your output.

○ Study your output. If you do not understand something there, look it up in the SPSS manuals or in a statistics book.

○ Learn to run SPSS using both pull-down menus and syntax files.

○ When debugging an SPSS program, first look at (and correct) the errors that occur early in your program.

DEVELOPING SKILLS

○ Think of the SPSS manuals as your friends, and refer to them often.

○ Take the next steps to becoming a more advanced SPSS user.

○ Have fun.

References

Einspruch, E. L. (2004). *Next steps with SPSS.* Thousand Oaks, CA: Sage.

Gibbons, J. D. (1985). *Nonparametric methods for quantitative analysis* (2nd ed.). Columbus, OH: American Sciences Press.

Gibbons, J. D. (1993). *Nonparametric statistics: An introduction.* Thousand Oaks, CA: Sage.

Gibbons, J. D., & Chakraborti, S. (1992). *Nonparametric statistical inference.* New York: Marcel Dekker.

Hays, W. (1991). *Statistics* (5th ed.). Orlando, FL: Harcourt Brace Jovanovich.

Iversen, G. R., & Norpoth, H. (1987). *Analysis of variance.* Thousand Oaks, CA: Sage.

Kanji, G. K. (1993). *100 statistical tests.* Thousand Oaks, CA: Sage.

Kirk, R. E. (1995). *Experimental design: Procedures for the behavioral sciences* (3rd ed.). Pacific Grove, CA: Brooks/Cole.

Lewis-Beck, M. S. (1980). *Applied regression: An introduction.* Thousand Oaks, CA: Sage.

Lewis-Beck, M. S. (1995). *Data analysis: An introduction.* Thousand Oaks, CA: Sage.

Pedhazur, E. (1997). *Multiple regression in behavioral research: Explanation and prediction* (3rd ed.). Orlando, FL: Harcourt Brace Jovanovich.

Schroeder, L. D., Sjoquist, D. L., & Stephan, P. E. (1986). *Understanding regression analysis: An introductory guide.* Thousand Oaks, CA: Sage.

Sirkin, R. M. (1999). *Statistics for the social sciences* (2nd ed.). Thousand Oaks, CA: Sage.

SPSS, Inc. (2003a). *SPSS base 12.0 user's guide.* Chicago: SPSS, Inc.

SPSS, Inc. (2003b). *SPSS 12.0 command syntax reference.* Chicago: SPSS, Inc.

SPSS, Inc. (2003c). *SPSS advanced modules 12.0.* Chicago: SPSS, Inc.

Index

About the Author

Eric L. Einspruch is a Senior Research Associate at RMC Research Corporation in Portland, Oregon. He received his BA from The Evergreen State College in Olympia, Washington, and he received his MSEd in counseling psychology and his PhD in educational research and evaluation from the University of Miami in Coral Gables, Florida. Much of his experience with large-scale data analysis was gained working in the Office of Institutional Research at Miami-Dade Community College. He has taught courses in statistical methods and in computer applications in educational research. He is currently involved in the evaluation of school-based and community-based social service programs, and he directs large-scale surveys. His publications have appeared in the *Florida Journal of Educational Research, International Journal of Early Childhood, Journal of Counseling Psychology, Journal of Primary Prevention, Journal of Drug Education, Psychotherapy in Private Practice, and Reaching Today's Youth.* He is also a backcountry skiing and mountaineering enthusiast.